JUN – – 2007

Custer's
Last Stand

Other books in the At Issue in History series:

The Attack on Pearl Harbor
The Battle of Gettysburg
The Bill of Rights
The Conquest of the New World
The Crash of 1929
The Cuban Missile Crisis
The Discovery of the AIDS Virus
The Indian Reservation System
Japanese American Internment Camps
The McCarthy Hearings
The Nuremberg Trials
Reconstruction
The Salem Witch Trials
The Sinking of the Titanic
The Tiananmen Square Massacre
The Treaty of Versailles

Custer's Last Stand

Thomas Streissguth, *Book Editor*

Daniel Leone, *President*
Bonnie Szumski, *Publisher*
Scott Barbour, *Managing Editor*

 **AT ISSUE IN HISTORY**

**GREENHAVEN
PRESS®**

San Diego • Detroit • New York • San Francisco • Cleveland
New Haven, Conn. • Waterville, Maine • London • Munich

© 2003 by Greenhaven Press. Greenhaven Press is an imprint of The Gale Group, Inc., a division of Thomson Learning, Inc.

Greenhaven® and Thomson Learning™ are trademarks used herein under license.

For more information, contact
Greenhaven Press
27500 Drake Rd.
Farmington Hills, MI 48331-3535
Or you can visit our Internet site at http://www.gale.com

Cover credit: © Stock Montage
Dover Publications, 12, 92
Library of Congress, 128
North Wind Picture Archives, 107

LIBRARY OF CONGRESS CATALOGING-IN-PUBLICATION DATA

Custer's last stand / Thomas Streissguth, book editor.
   p. cm. — (At issue in history)
Includes bibliographical references and index.
ISBN 0-7377-1359-3 (pbk. : alk. paper) — ISBN 0-7377-1358-5 (hc. : alk. paper)
   1. Little Bighorn, Battle of the, Mont., 1876. I. Streissguth, Thomas, 1958– .
II. Series.
E83.876 .C9864 2003
973.8'2—dc21
                                               2002027875

Printed in the United States of America

Contents

Foreword   8

Introduction   10

Chapter 1: Contemporary Accounts and Explanations

1. Early Dispatches from the Little Bighorn
   by the New York Times   20
   The bodies of Lieutenant Colonel George Arm-
   strong Custer and his men were discovered on
   June 27, 1876, two days after the battle. A horrified
   audience read the news brought east by dispatch
   rider and telegraph. Early newspaper accounts,
   such as this one offered in the *New York Times*, provided few details but much lurid speculation.

2. A Failed Indian Policy Caused Custer's Defeat
   by Harper's Weekly   28
   During the summer of 1876, journalists, military
   men, and government officials worked hard to
   assign, or avoid, blame for the Little Bighorn
   disaster. One essay in *Harper's Weekly*, a leading
   journal of social and political commentary, put the
   blame squarely on the U.S. government's policy of
   making, then breaking, treaties with the Indians.

3. A Cavalryman at the Little Bighorn
   by William O. Taylor   31
   The men attached to Major Marcus Reno's com-
   mand were ordered to make a direct assault on an
   immense Indian village, where they were outnumbered, outflanked, and quickly thrown back.
   Private William O. Taylor recounts the confusing
   fight and the near-panic that gripped the battalion as the men of his company hastily retreated
   across the Little Bighorn to safety.

4. Custer Was Betrayed by Reno and Benteen
   by Frederick Whittaker   41
   In the general public opinion, George A. Custer,
   a cavalry officer who had won many engagements

for the North during the Civil War, epitomized the best qualities of the U.S. military: boldness, courage under fire, and personal charisma. Writing immediately after the defeat at the Little Bighorn, an admiring author speculates on Custer's heroic exploits in the last hours of his life.

5. I Did My Duty at the Little Bighorn
   by Marcus Reno   51
   An official court of inquiry into the Battle of the Little Bighorn was convened in Chicago in January 1879—too late for an official court-martial. The star witness of this inquiry, Major Marcus Reno, defends himself against charges that he panicked on Reno Hill and failed to come to Custer's support when his battalion was needed.

Chapter 2: The Last Stand Through Indian Eyes

1. Cheyenne Warriors Recall the Little Bighorn Battle *by George Bird Grinnell*   61
   For the warriors who fought against Custer at the Little Bighorn, a golden opportunity had finally come to prove their mettle and defeat the horse soldiers who had been making war against their people for so many years. Several Cheyenne warriors describe the events leading up to the battle and their personal experiences on the battlefield.

2. The Sioux and Cheyenne Won Through Superior Leadership *by James Welch*   73
   The stories of Indian warriors who experienced the Battle of the Little Bighorn, and evidence found at the battlefield, show that the Indians fought with great valor while Custer's men panicked and fought ineffectively.

3. The Sioux and Cheyenne Perspective on the Battle *by Dee Brown*   88
   White settlement on the plains may have been haphazard, but the campaign against the Indians was a carefully planned process of deception and massacre. Custer's defeat turned out to be one moment of triumph and glory for the Indians

who had suffered a long string of defeats and humiliation.

Chapter 3: The Modern Analysis

1. The Tactics of Custer and Crazy Horse
by Stephen E. Ambrose   98
The Sioux campaign of 1876 was a carefully
planned and complex operation that, considering
Custer's previous experiences on the plains, had
every chance of succeeding. But Custer overlooked the many aspects of the tactical situation
that put him at a disadvantage. In this account of
the maneuvers taken by the Seventh Cavalry
before the battle, the author describes Custer's
ill-fated, overconfident decisions.

2. Custer Could Have Won the Battle
by Robert M. Utley   111
None of Custer's battalion survived the Battle of
the Little Bighorn, and as a result the true nature
and course of the battle have been debated since
the last shot was fired. The author summarizes
the many controversies surrounding the battle,
analyzes the actions taken by Custer, and concludes that Custer did in fact make sound decisions that day.

3. Envy and Pique Motivated Captain Benteen
by Larry Sklenar   121
The actions of Captain Frederick Benteen, who
was ordered away from the main force on a
reconnaissance mission by Custer, have attracted
heavy criticism from historians of the battle.
Author Larry Sklenar believes Benteen felt
slighted by Custer's orders. Carefully analyzing
Benteen's actions and his later explanations for
those actions, he faults Benteen for acting out of
sheer envy of Custer's national renown.

For Further Research   136

Index   138

Foreword

Historian Robert Weiss defines history simply as "a record and interpretation of past events." Both elements—record and interpretation—are necessary, Weiss argues.

Names, dates, places, and events are the essence of history. But historical writing is not a compendium of facts. It consists of facts placed in a sequence to tell a connected story. A work of history is not merely a story, however. It also must analyze what happened and *why*—that is, it must interpret the past for the reader.

For example, the events of December 7, 1941, that led President Franklin D. Roosevelt to call it "a date which will live in infamy" are fairly well known and straightforward. A force of Japanese planes and submarines launched a torpedo and bombing attack on American military targets in Pearl Harbor, Hawaii. The surprise assault sank five battleships, disabled or sank fourteen additional ships, and left almost twenty-four hundred American soldiers and sailors dead. On the following day, the United States formally entered World War II when Congress declared war on Japan.

These facts and consequences were almost immediately communicated to the American people who heard reports about Pearl Harbor and President Roosevelt's response on the radio. All realized that this was an important and pivotal event in American and world history. Yet the news from Pearl Harbor raised many unanswered questions. Why did Japan decide to launch such an offensive? Why were the attackers so successful in catching America by surprise? What did the attack reveal about the two nations, their people, and their leadership? What were its causes, and what were its effects? Political leaders, academic historians, and students look to learn the basic facts of historical events and to read the intepretations of these events by many different sources, both primary and secondary, in order to develop a more complete picture of the event in a historical context.

In the case of Pearl Harbor, several important questions surrounding the event remain in dispute, most notably the role of President Roosevelt. Some historians have blamed his policies for deliberately provoking Japan to attack in order to propel America into World War II; a few have gone so far as to accuse him of knowing of the impending attack but not informing others. Other historians, examining the same event, have exonerated the president of such charges, arguing that the historical evidence does not support such a theory.

The Greenhaven At Issue in History series recognizes that many important historical events have been interpreted differently and in some cases remain shrouded in controversy. Each volume features a collection of articles that focus on a topic that has sparked controversy among eyewitnesses, contemporary observers, and historians. An introductory essay sets the stage for each topic by presenting background and context. Several chapters then examine different facets of the subject at hand with readings chosen for their diversity of opinion. Each selection is preceded by a summary of the author's main points and conclusions. A bibliography is included for those students interested in pursuing further research. An annotated table of contents and thorough index help readers to quickly locate material of interest. Taken together, the contents of each of the volumes in the Greenhaven At Issue in History series will help students become more discriminating and thoughtful readers of history.

Introduction

In the rolling plains of Indian Territory, in what is now the state of Oklahoma, the November nights were cold, windy, desolate, and dangerous. On one such night—November 26, 1868—a young cavalry officer, Lieutenant Colonel George Armstrong Custer, led 720 men of the U.S. Seventh Cavalry along a curving trail recently traveled by a large group of Indians. In search of food, weapons, and trade goods, and to drive away settlers crossing frontier territory ceded by treaty, the Indians of the Great Plains were raiding wagon trains, settlements, train depots, and isolated homesteads north into Kansas. One Plains tribe was moving south into Indian Territory to make their winter camp along the Washita River.

Custer was not yet sure of who, exactly, he was pursuing. His orders were to fight hostile Indians wherever he might find them, and to teach a stern lesson about the consequences of raiding white settlements, homesteads, and wagon trains. Major General Philip Sheridan had selected Custer for this operation in spite of Custer's many troubles with his fellow officers and a recent court-martial. The lieutenant colonel was undisciplined, mischievous, and mercurial, Sheridan knew, but Custer was also a brilliant tactician and a man with unbounded enthusiasm for the difficult task at hand.

Well after dark, Custer and his troops reached the banks of the Washita, where Custer called a halt and gave orders for an attack at first light. He divided the battalion into four, sending one of the columns all the way around to the opposite side of the village, two more to either side, and one in front. He would catch the village by surprise and attack from all four directions at once.

The Battle of the Washita took place at dawn on November 27, 1868. As Custer's troops galloped through the village, Indian warriors ran from their lodges, loading and firing their rifles. They fought with great bravery, but without their horses, which were tethered outside of the camp, they had a poor chance of fighting on equal terms. Many were killed within the village, while others fled to the banks of the Washita or into the shallows of the river for cover. Terrified women, older men, and children scattered into the surrounding hills. Many of them were shot down, as Custer's men took no prisoners and made no distinction between combatants and noncombatants. In a very short time, the battle was over.

Custer's command had suffered few casualties—only one officer was killed—and had inflicted a terrible defeat on a village of Cheyenne, led by a chief named Black Kettle, who was slain in the first moments of the battle. Custer gave orders to burn the village, allow one horse each for the survivors, and shoot the several hundred horses that remained. He had no supplies to feed these horses and did not want the Indians to recover them. Custer and his men regretted this cold-blooded slaughter, but war on the plains was like that: pitiless and tragic for animals as well as human beings. Though he did not know it at the time, his tactics at the Washita would play an important role in Custer's ultimate fate.

George Armstrong Custer

With the victory at the Washita, Custer had rescued his reputation and his good name in the army. He had very recently been a disgraced officer, court-martialed for leaving his command. Now, once again, he was a hero and a man admired in the military and among the civilian population.

George Armstrong Custer was born on December 5, 1839, in New Rumley, Ohio, the son of Emmanuel Custer and his second wife, Matilda Viers. The family included eleven children from this and previous marriages. "Autie," as he was nicknamed, had moved as a boy to the home of his half sister, Lydia, in Monroe, Michigan, then two years later moved back to New Rumley. He worked as a teacher after graduating from school at sixteen, but his ambitions lay well beyond the humdrum life of a schoolmaster. He saw a chance for a better future in the U.S. Army and at the military academy at West Point, New York. Although his family were Democrats, Custer secured the necessary appointment from his Republican congressman, John Bingham, and enrolled at West Point in July 1857. Disciplined many times for various minor infractions, he managed to graduate, although at the bottom of his class, in the spring of 1861.

The Seventh Cavalry attacked the Cheyenne at the Battle of the Washita. The Cheyenne were caught off guard and suffered massive losses.

It was an eventful time for the United States. Seven southern states had seceded from the Union over the threat posed to southern institutions, including slavery, by the Republican administration of President Abraham Lincoln. In April 1861, a battery of guns under the control of a southern officer opened fire on Fort Sumter, a federal fortification lying in Charleston Harbor. The Civil War between North and South, and between Union and Confederate armies, had begun.

Custer was no abolitionist and no Republican. As a northern Democrat, he felt strong sympathy for the Southerners and their cause. But Custer saw his duty and his future in the Union army. He served first as a staff officer with General George McClellan, the leader of the Army of the Potomac, the Union's eastern army. After McClellan was dismissed by President Lincoln in the spring of 1863, Custer was appointed as an aide to General Alfred Pleasanton, a divisional cavalry commander in the Army of the Potomac. In the summer of 1863, Custer was appointed a brigadier general, head of the Second Brigade of Michigan cavalry volunteers. Throughout the war, Custer earned the respect of his superior officers with his energy, courage in battle, and unhesitating obedience. His valor and success also earned him popular acclaim in the civilian world. At the conclusion of the Civil War, Custer was one of the best-known officers in the victorious Union army.

But the end of the war left Custer at loose ends. His fame and success might have led to a successful political career, but he had no taste for the give-and-take and constant intrigue and compromises that came with a political career. He decided to remain in the army and seek his future where he felt most at home: in an officer's quarters and on the battlefield, wherever he might find it.

The army sent Custer west to assist in defeating the remaining pockets of Confederate resistance and to subdue the Plains Indians, who still lived a nomadic life of hunting on the vast, nearly treeless tablelands between the Mississippi River and the Rocky Mountains. Custer was first posted as an aide to General Philip Sheridan during an expedition to Texas. In 1867, he joined the Seventh Cavalry at Fort Riley, Kansas. It was during this posting that Custer scored his first great success on the plains, his victory over Black Kettle's Cheyenne village on the Washita River.

The war on the plains was proceeding as a series of small, short battles, separated by long periods of truce. While white settlers moved west along the trails between the plains and the mountains, Cheyenne, Sioux, and other native peoples saw their hunting grounds invaded and the buffalo they depended on for food, clothing, and shelter gradually disappear. Every few years, a new treaty was signed between the Indians and the U.S. government, as both sides tried to stake out their respective territories and rights. Inevitably, as settlement continued on the plains, and as new railroads, towns, and farms were created, the treaties were broken, and war began anew.

In the years after the Civil War, a series of cavalry forts along the Bozeman Trail, in Wyoming and Montana territories, had come under attack by hostile Sioux, and a series of defeats had been inflicted on the proud U.S. Cavalry. The fighting and the losses persuaded the U.S. government that another treaty would be needed. As a result, several months before the Battle of the Washita, the Sioux and the United States had signed the Fort Laramie agreement. The treaty allowed the Sioux to keep the territory between the Black Hills of Dakota Territory and the Missouri River as land reserved for their own use and settlement. Farther west, between the Black Hills and the Bighorn Mountains of

Wyoming, the Sioux would have an open range of land, or "unceded" territory, in which to carry out their annual buffalo hunts. The cavalry forts would be abandoned, and the Bozeman Trail would be closed to the white hunters, settlers, and miners who used it.

After the Fort Laramie treaty was signed, the Sioux began moving to reservation agencies, where they were expected to settle down in permanent homes. They would be supplied with food and other necessities and with the seed and necessary tools to become productive farmers and livestock herders. The Indians were expected to leave behind thousands of years of their customary nomadic life and transform themselves in the image of white farmers and settlers.

Many Sioux tried to accept this new and unfamiliar life, but many others would not. Among them were two prestigious chiefs named Crazy Horse and Sitting Bull, who counted themselves among the "hostiles"—those Indians who would not accept farming or settlement and lived by the old nomadic ways.

Although both chiefs were widely admired among the Sioux, by 1875 the agency population vastly outnumbered the hostiles who were living away from the reservations. There simply were not enough buffalo and not enough open range left to support the entire Sioux nation. Yet the agencies were places of misery where ill-clad Indians existed on the brink of starvation, depending on government handouts and subject to thieving, corrupt agents.

In the spring of 1876, thousands of reservation Sioux returned to the hunting grounds along the Powder River, in eastern Wyoming and Montana. They were goaded on by Sitting Bull and Crazy Horse, both of whom sent an open invitation to their followers to gather for a traditional buffalo hunt. A huge encampment began to form on the banks of Rosebud Creek, a tributary of the Yellowstone River. Sioux and Cheyenne from throughout the northern plains arrived to set up their lodges, collect a vast herd of ponies, and join in the hunt for buffalo. The Indians sought safety in numbers, for they knew an important and decisive fight would be coming that summer.

The Sioux Expedition

Determined to stop this exodus from the agencies and to herd all of the hostiles back to the reservations or wipe them out entirely, the U.S. Army began planning a military campaign into the Powder River country. The expedition would attack from the north and south, catching the hostiles between two large forces of cavalry. One of the columns would be led by Colonel John Gibbon, who would proceed down the Yellowstone River from the west. General Alfred Terry would command the second and largest column, which would start out from Fort Abraham Lincoln in what is now North Dakota and travel up the Yellowstone from the east. Riding in Terry's column were Lieutenant Colonel Custer's twelve troops of the Seventh Cavalry. The third column, that of General George Crook, would proceed north from Forth Fetterman in Wyoming. According to the plan, Terry's and Gibbon's columns would join along the Yellowstone, move south, and catch the Sioux between themselves and General Crook.

On June 10, 1876, the Terry and Gibbon columns met at the mouth of Rosebud Creek. They had not yet found the Sioux village, but they had concluded that the hostiles were camped along one of the river valleys to the south. They were correct: The village was moving between the Rosebud and Little Bighorn valleys. By this time, it numbered as many as ten thousand people, with as many as three thousand warriors among them.

On June 17, General Crook's southern column met a party of Sioux warriors led by Crazy Horse along upper Rosebud Creek. The battle seesawed for several hours, with the bold Sioux swooping down on troopers fighting in the unsheltered hills rising from the creek valley. Finally, Crook managed to drive the Indians from the field of battle, but he would proceed no farther down the Rosebud, and he would not join with Gibbon or Terry. The Battle of the Rosebud turned out to be a victory for Crazy Horse, who drove the southern column back.

In the meantime, Custer had sent Major Marcus Reno of the Seventh Cavalry on a scout for the Sioux. Reno exceeded orders by going all the way to Rosebud Creek. He had found a trail leading off to the west in the direction of the Little Bighorn River, but instead of following this trail, he had returned down the Tongue River to headquarters. Custer immediately confronted and berated Reno for abandoning the trail.

Custer and Reno were not fond of each other, nor did

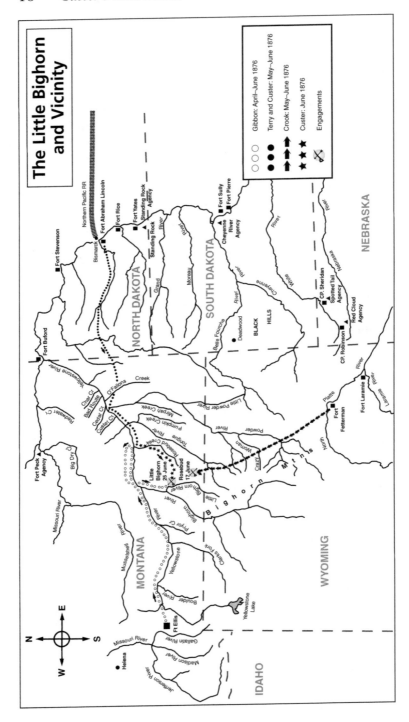

The Little Bighorn and Vicinity

Custer get along with another officer serving under him, Captain Frederick Benteen. This campaign carried with it a strong undercurrent of envy and personal ambition among the Seventh Cavalry officers, all of whom knew a victory in the coming battle would bring them high honors, and for Custer, very possibly a bid for the Democratic candidacy for president in the fall. To Reno and Benteen, Custer was little more than a skillful glory hunter. Custer's overconfidence, and the jealousy and rivalry among the three men, would lead to disaster in less than a week.

After Reno's return, General Terry moved his headquarters up to the mouth of the Rosebud, where the officers met on the river steamboat *Far West.* Terry asked Custer to take his force up the Rosebud, then march cross-country to the Little Bighorn in search of the encampment. Gibbon would return up the Yellowstone to the mouth of the Little Bighorn, then go up the Little Bighorn to try to find the Indians on his own. Although Terry offered the use of four extra cavalry troops and four Gatling guns, Custer refused them. In his opinion, the guns would only slow him down. He was confident that with the element of surprise and the army's superior firepower, he could whip any force of Indians on the plains.

Custer left the *Far West* and the Yellowstone River on June 22. He led his troops up the Rosebud and two days later headed directly west, toward the valley of the Little Bighorn. A large trail indicated that the village had passed this way. Custer would follow it and catch the Indians as quickly as possible. On the night of June 24, he continued marching, his troops growing fatigued. After a few hours of sleep, Custer's battalion arose early on the morning of June 25, when the Indian scouts serving with Custer finally spotted the huge encampment on the west bank of the Little Bighorn River. The scouts warned Custer that he was about to encounter the largest Indian village they had ever seen. Custer disregarded their warnings.

Later that day, the scout Charley Varnum reported that the Indians might be moving away—the event that Custer feared the most. Sioux scouts from the village had been spotted, and Custer believed they were already giving the warning of the Seventh Cavalry's approach. Instead of preparing for an attack the next day, Custer decided to attack immediately. He split the column into three battalions, led by Benteen, Reno, and himself. Fatigued by the long march and the hot weather, the men of the Seventh Cavalry marched directly toward the valley of the Little Bighorn and the Last Stand of General Custer, whose force of five cavalry troops, 211 men in all, would be met and wiped out by sundown.

The events that occurred on the afternoon of June 25, 1876, have been a fruitful field of debate for historians ever since. Several questions have dominated this debate: Why did Custer split his column in three just before doing battle with an immense force of Indian warriors? Why did Major Reno and Captain Benteen not come to Custer's aid, even when they received messages from their commanding officer to come immediately and to bring ammunition? How exactly did Custer proceed after the force was split, and how did the Sioux leader Crazy Horse and the Indians defeat him? Was the outcome due to Custer's ineptness and over-confidence or to superior tactics on the part of the Indians? What would have been the outcome of the battle had Custer held the Seventh Cavalry together?

Because not a single man in Custer's battalion survived the Last Stand, this event stands out as one of the most intriguing and fascinating in the history of the Plains Indian wars. It also represents the high tide of history for the Sioux Indians, who would never again score such an important victory and whose roaming life on the plains would soon come to an end. In many ways, Custer's Last Stand represents, in miniature, the entire fascinating history of plains warfare and played a crucial role in its ultimately tragic outcome.

Chapter 1

Contemporary Accounts and Explanations

1

Early Dispatches from the Little Bighorn

New York Times

The news of Custer's defeat traveled by dispatch rider back to Fort Lincoln, the Seventh Cavalry post in the northern Dakota Territory, and thence by telegraph to news outlets in Bismarck, Chicago, and New York. Although the U.S. Army officially confirmed the grim story, journalists throughout the nation speculated on Custer's actions and the reasons for his defeat. A new, more serious era in the war with the Plains Indians was beginning, one in which many editorialists would call for a campaign of total war to avenge the deaths of Custer and his men.

The *New York Times* used several dispatches in the following lengthy front-page story, which ran on July 6, 1876, nearly two weeks after the battle. Sketchy details of Custer's movements toward the Little Bighorn and of his rash advance on a huge Indian encampment were followed by criticism of the Sioux campaign of 1876 and the weak support given the army by the U.S. Congress. As was common practice at the time, the *Times* mixed news, speculation, opinion, and hyperbole, all in an effort to stir the emotions of the reader and whet the public's appetite for the next day's edition.

LATEST ACCOUNTS OF THE CHARGE. FORCE OF FOUR THOUSAND INDIANS IN POSITION ATTACKED BY LESS THAN FOUR HUNDRED TROOPS—OPINIONS OF LEADING ARMY OFFICERS OF THE DEED AND ITS CONSEQUENCES—FEELING IN THE COMMUNITY OVER THE DISASTER.

Excerpted from "The Little Big Horn Massacre," *New York Times*, July 6, 1876.

The dispatches giving an account of the slaughter of Gen. Custer's command, published in the *Times* of yesterday, are confirmed and supplemented by official reports from Gen. A.H. Terry, commanding the expedition. On June 25 Gen. Custer's command came upon the main camp of Sitting Bull, and at once attacked it, charging the thickest part of it with five companies, Major [Marcus] Reno, with seven companies attacking on the other side. The soldiers were repulsed and a wholesale slaughter ensued. Gen. Custer, his brother, his nephew, and his brother-in-law were killed, and not one of his detachment escaped. The Indians surrounded Major Reno's command and held them in the hills during a whole day, but [Major General John] Gibbon's command came up and the Indians left. The number of killed is stated at 300 and the wounded at 31. Two hundred and seven men are said to have been buried in one place. The list of killed includes seventeen commissioned officers.

It is the opinion of Army officers in Chicago, Washington, and Philadelphia, including Gens. [William T.] Sherman and [Philip] Sheridan, that Gen. Custer was rashly imprudent to attack such a large number of Indians, Sitting Bull's force being 4,000 strong. Gen. Sherman thinks that the accounts of the disaster are exaggerated. The wounded soldiers are being conveyed to Fort Lincoln. Additional details are anxiously awaited throughout the country.

Confirmation of the Disaster

DISPATCHES FROM GEN. TERRY RECEIVED AT SHERIDAN'S HEADQUARTERS. THEORIES OF THE BATTLE—PROBABLY TEN THOUSAND SIOUX IN POSITION—THE ATTACK CONDEMNED AS RASH BY OFFICERS OF EXPERIENCE—DISPOSITION OF THE WOUNDED.

Chicago, July 6.—At the headquarters of Lieut. Gen. Sheridan this morning, all was bustle and confusion over the reported massacre of Custer's command. Telegrams were being constantly received, but most of them were of a confidential nature and withheld from publication. It is known that the unfortunate command broke camp on the North Rosebud [Creek] on June 22 for the purpose of proceeding in a direction which would bring it to the point named about the 25th, at which place a bloody fight is reported to have taken time. The following dispatch, the last received at headquarters in this city previous to the news of the massacre, confirms the accounts given to the extent of showing that Custer intended to go to that place.

Camp on the North Rosebud, June 21, 1876.

Lieut. Gen. P.H. Sheridan, Commanding Military Division of the Missouri, Chicago: No Indians have been met with as yet, but traces of large and recent camp have been discovered twenty or thirty miles up the Rosebud. Gibbon's column will move this morning, on the north side of the Yellowstone, for the mouth of the Big Horn, where it will be ferried across by the supply steamer, and whence it will proceed to the mouth of the Little [Big] Horn, and so on. Custer will go up the Rosebud tomorrow with his whole regiment, and thence to the headwaters of the Little Horn, thence down the Little Horn.

A.H. TERRY,

Brigadier General Commanding.

A dispatch received at the quarters of Gen. Sheridan this morning at 11 o'clock confirms the first reports received. The dispatch states that the forces were falling back, and that the wounded had been sent to Fort Lincoln. No details were given, but the officers at headquarters regard it as a full confirmation of the engagement reported. In reply to an inquiry as to whether the attack was made by Gen. Custer of his own accord, or under orders from the department, an answer was given that Custer made the charge of his own volition. A still later dispatch from Lieut. [John] Kinzie, of the Seventh Cavalry, was received asking that he be transferred from the department where he is now on duty to the scene of action. This is also regarded as another confirmation of the bloody massacre reported. Gen. Custer's family are at Fort Lincoln, to which point the wounded are being conveyed.

So far as an expression in regard to the wisdom of Gen. Custer's attack could be obtained at headquarters, it was to the effect that Custer had been imprudent, to say the least. It is the opinion at headquarters among those who are most familiar with the situation, that Custer struck Sitting Bull's main camp. Gen. [R.C.] Drum, of Sheridan's staff, is of [the] opinion that Sitting Bull began concentrating his forces after the fight with [General George] Crook [on June 17 at the Rosebud], and that no doubt, Custer dropped squarely into the midst of no less than ten thousand red devils and was literally torn to pieces. The movement made by Custer is censured to some extent at military headquarters in this city. The older officers say that it was brought about by that foolish pride which so often results in the defeat of men. It seems that a few days before Gen. Terry had offered four additional companies to Custer, but that officer refused them.

The information at headquarters further is to the effect that Gen. Gibbon with his force was known to be moving up to Custer for the purpose of reinforcing him; and that he knew of this, and knew that Gibbon would arrive by the following day after the engagement. I have it on as good authority as one of the leading officers at headquarters, that Custer had been ordered by Terry to make a march toward the Little Big Horn and to form a junction with a column of infantry that was moving diagonally across the country to the same point. The two columns were then to cooperate and make an attack. Instead of marching from twenty to thirty miles per day, as ordered, Custer made a forced march and reached the point of destination two or three days in advance of the infantry; then finding himself in front of the foe he foolishly attempted to out his way through and punish the red devils.

Details of the Battle

GRAPHIC DESCRIPTION OF THE FIGHTING—MAJOR RENO'S COMMAND UNDER FIRE FOR TWO DAYS—EVERY MAN OF CUSTER'S DETACHMENT KILLED EXCEPT ONE SCOUT—AFFECTING SCENES WHEN RELIEF ARRIVED.

Chicago, July 6.—A special to the *Times* tonight from Bismarck, recounts most graphically the late encounter with the Indians on the Little Big Horn. Gen. Custer left the Rosebud on June 22, with twelve companies of the Seventh Cavalry, striking a trail where Reno left it, leading in the direction of the Little Horn. On the evening of the 24th fresh trails were reported, and on the morning of the 25th an Indian village, twenty miles above the mouth of the Little Horn was reported about three miles long and half a mile wide and fifteen miles away. Custer pushed his command rapidly through. They had made a march of seventy-eight miles in twenty-four hours preceding the battle. When near the village it was discovered that the Indians were moving in hot haste as if retreating. Reno, with seven companies of the Seventh Cavalry, was ordered to the left to attack the village at its head, while Custer, with five companies, went to the right and commenced a vigorous attack. Reno fell on them with three companies of cavalry, and was almost instantly surrounded, and after one hour or more of vigorous fighting, during which he lost Lieuts. [Benjamin] Hodgson and [Donald] McIntosh and Dr. [James] Dewolf and twelve men, with several Indian scouts killed and many wounded, he cut his way through to the river and gained a bluff 300 feet in height, where he entrenched and was soon joined by Col. [Henry] Benson with four companies. In the meantime the Indians resumed the attack, making repeated and desperate charges, which were repulsed with great slaughter to the Indians. They gained higher ground than Reno occupied, and as their arms were longer range and better than the cavalry's, they kept up a galling fire until nightfall. During the night Reno strengthened his position, and was prepared for another attack, which was made at daylight.

The day wore on. Reno had lost in killed and wounded a large portion of his command, forty odd having been killed before the bluff was reached, many of them in hand to hand conflict with the Indians, who outnumbered them ten to one, and his men had been without water for thirty-six hours. The suffering was heartrending. In this state of affairs they determined to reach the water at all hazards, and Col. Benson made a sally with his company, and routed the main body of the Indians who were guarding the approach to the river. The Indian sharpshooters were nearly opposite the mouth of the ravine through which the brave boys approached the river, but the attempt was made, and though one man was killed and seven wounded the water was gained and the command relieved. When the fighting ceased for the night Reno further prepared for attacks.

There had been forty-eight hours' fighting, with no word from Custer. Twenty-four hours more of fighting and the suspense ended, when the Indians abandoned their village in great haste and confusion.

Reno knew then that succor was near at hand. Gen. Terry, with Gibbon commanding his own infantry, had arrived, and as the comrades met men wept on each other's necks. Inquiries were then made for Custer, but none could tell where he was. Soon an officer came rushing into camp and related that he had found Custer, dead, stripped naked, but not mutilated, and near him his two brothers, Col. Tom and Boston Custer. His brother-in-law, Col. Calhoun, and his nephew Col. [George] Yates, Col. [Miles] Keogh, Capt. Smith, Lieut. [John J.] Crittenden, Lieut. [Samuel] Sturgis,

Col. [William] Cooke, Lieut. [James] Porter, Lieut. [Henry] Harrington, Dr. Lord, Mark Kellogg, the Bismarck *Tribune* correspondent, and 190 men and scouts. Custer went into battle with Companies C, L, I, F, and E, of the Seventh Cavalry, and the staff and non-commissioned staff of his regiment and a number of scouts, and only one Crow scout remained to tell the tale. All are dead. Custer was surrounded on every side by Indians, and horses fell as they fought on skirmish line or in line of battle. Custer was among the last who fell, but when his cheering voice was no longer heard, the Indians made easy work of the remainder. The bodies of all save the newspaper correspondent were stripped, and most of them were horribly mutilated. Custer's was not mutilated. He was shot through the body and through the head. The troops cared for the wounded and buried the dead, and returned to their base for supplies and instructions from the General of the Army.

Col. Smith arrived at Bismarck last night with thirty-five of the wounded. The Indians lost heavily in the Battle. The Crow scout survived by hiding in a ravine. He believes the Indians lost more than the whites. The village numbered 1,800 lodges, and it is thought there were 4,000 warriors. Gen. Custer was directed by Gen. Terry to find . . . the Indians, but not to fight unless Terry arrived with infantry and with Gibbon's column.

The Causes and the Consequences

FRUITS OF THE ILL-ADVISED BLACK HILLS EXPEDITION OF TWO YEARS AGO—ABILITY OF THE ARMY TO RENEW OPERATIONS EFFECTIVELY DISCUSSED—THE PERSONNEL OF THE CHARGING PARTY STILL UNDEFINED.

Washington, July 6.—The news of the fatal charge of Gen. Custer and his command against the Sioux Indians has caused great excitement in Washington, particularly among Army people and about the Capitol. The first impulse was to doubt the report, or set it down as some heartless hoax or at least a greatly exaggerated story by some frightened fugitive. At the second thought the report was generally accepted as true in its chief and appalling incidents. The campaign against the wild Sioux was undertaken under disadvantageous circumstances owing to the refusal of Congress to appropriate money for the establishment of military posts on the upper Yellowstone River. Gen. Sherman and

Gen. Sheridan both asked for these posts, which, in case of anticipated troubles would give the troops a base of supplies about four hundred miles nearer the hostile country than they could otherwise have. The posts desired would have been accessible by steamboats on the Yellowstone, which would have conveyed men and supplies. The House Committee on Military Affairs unanimously recommended their establishment, but the Committee on Appropriations refused to provide in their bills the necessary means. This is regarded as the immediate cause of the disaster. The remote cause was undoubtedly the expedition into the Black Hills two years ago in violation of laws and treaties, authorized by Secretary [of War William] Belknap and led by Gen. Custer. If there had been a post at the head of navigation on the Yellowstone the expedition would doubtless have proceeded thence against the Indians in one invincible column. The policy of sending three converging columns so many hundred miles against such brave and skillful soldiers as the Sioux has been the cause of some uneasiness here among the few who have taken the trouble to think about the facts and prospects. The Sioux seem to have understood clearly the plan of attack, and threw themselves with their whole force first against Gen. Crook's column and now against Custer's, and both times inflicted serious disaster. The feeling was common today that the campaign is a failure, and that there must follow a general Indian war, promising to be costly in men and money. The Sioux are a distinct race of men from the so-called Indians of the Southwest, among whom the army found such easy work two and three years ago. The Sioux live by the chase and feed chiefly upon flesh.

The Southern Indians are farmers and eat fruits and vegetables, the latter are at their worst cruel, cowardly robbers. The former are as much like the brave and warlike red men represented by [William Fenimore Cooper's novel] *The Last of the Mohicans* as ever existed outside the covers of fiction and romance. This difference between the foes in the North and Southwest seems not to have been well counted upon, nor provided for, and formed, as it might, prudently, no restraint upon the reckless fatal charge of the 300. If the tale told by the courier . . . is true, the charge has scarce a parallel in the history of civilized or savage warfare.

The massacre of Major [Frances] Dade and his command in the Florida [Seminole] war is alone comparable with it in American history. The reason for an expedition against the Indians this Summer is not well understood, nor has any satisfactory explanation been published. The wild Sioux had never been willing to live upon the reservations marked out for them, and the understanding has been that they were to be whipped into submission, and compelled to live like [Indian chiefs] Red Cloud and Spotted Tail, with their bands, about the Government agencies. The question of the policy and right of the war will now be renewed and discussed, and, indeed, is discussed today. Those who believe in the policy of the extermination of the Indians, and think the speedier the better its accomplishment, look upon the condition of war as inevitable, and are for pouring thousands of troops into the Indian country and giving them a terrible punishment. This class is small, even in the Army, where the policy of extermination is not popular save with a few high and restless officers. The invasion of the Black Hills has been condemned over and over again by the peace party, and there are very many who can truthfully say, "I told you so." From that unwarranted invasion the present difficulties have gradually sprung up, so that an expedition that originally cost a hundred thousand dollars perhaps, must lead to an expenditure of millions, which will advance civilization in no way, except by the destruction of the uncivilized. The Army, if the present campaign wholly fails, is in no condition to renew hostilities with sufficient force, and there is little reason to expect Congress will this session provide for an Indian war. Thus by force of circumstances a continuation of the war would probably be with the Government forces upon the defensive, protecting as far as possible agencies and settlements. There is another result that some hope for. It is the union of the three columns of troops and the delivery of a blow against the Indians that will place them at the mercy of the Army and compel them to sue for peace. The chances are, however, so far as the information now at hand may be relied on, that the Government forces are much too small in number, reduced as they are by two battles, to meet the powerful and exultant Sioux.

2

A Failed Indian Policy Caused Custer's Defeat

Harper's Weekly

Debate and recrimination raged through the summer of 1876 as the public learned the full details of the disaster at the Little Bighorn. Whereas some faulted a weak-kneed government policy that coddled Indians on comfortable reservations and refused to provide the army with the men and material it needed, others pointed to the long-standing policy of making, then breaking, treaties with the Plains Indians.

Harper's Weekly, then a leading journal of literary and political criticism, came down on the latter side of the debate. Although the editorial of August 5, 1876, excerpted here, recognized the gallantry and skill of General Custer, the writer also points out the hypocrisy of promising the Sioux and other Plains tribes the free use of their lands and then allowing settlers and prospectors to break the pledges made by Indian agents and commissioners. The editorial concludes that a more intelligent and forthright policy toward the "savages" might prevent another last stand.

The fate of the brave and gallant Custer has deeply touched the public heart, which sees only a fearless soldier leading a charge against an ambushed foe, and falling at the head of his men and in the thick of the fray. A monument is proposed, and subscriptions have been made. But a truer monument, more enduring than brass or marble, would be an Indian policy intelligent, moral, and efficient. Custer would not have fallen in vain if such a policy should

From "The Custer Massacre," *Harper's Weekly*, August 5, 1876.

be the result of his death. It is a permanent accusation against our humanity and ability that over the Canadian line the relations between the Indians and whites are so tranquil, while upon our side they are summed up in perpetual treachery, waste, and war. When he was a young lieutenant on the frontier, General [Ulysses S.] Grant saw this, and watching attentively, he came to the conclusion that the reason of the difference was that the English respected the rights of the Indians and kept faith with them, while we make solemn treaties with them as if they were civilized and powerful nations, and then practically regard them as vermin to be exterminated. The folly of making treaties with the Indian tribes may be as great as treating with a herd of buffalo. But the infamy of violating treaties when we have made them is undeniable, and we are guilty both of the folly and the infamy.

We make treaties—that is, we pledge our faith—and then leave swindlers and knaves of all kinds to execute them. We maintain and breed pauper colonies. The savages who know us and who will neither be pauperized nor trust our word we pursue and slay if we can at an incredible expense. The flower of our young officers is lost in inglorious forays, and one of the intelligent students of the whole subject rises in Congress and says, "The fact is that these Indians, with whom we have made a solemn treaty that their territory should not be invaded, and that they should receive supplies upon their reservations, have seen from one thousand to fifteen hundred miners during the present season entering and occupying their territory, while the Indians, owing to the failure of this and the last Congress to make adequate appropriations for their subsistence, instead of being fattened, as the gentleman says, by the support of the government, have simply been starved." The Red Cloud investigation of last year [a congressional investigation into corruption among agents responsible for supplying and managing Sioux reservations in what is now Nebraska], however inadequate, sufficed to show the practice under our Indian policy, and we regretted then that ex-Governor [Alexander H.] Bullock of Massachusetts declined the appointment upon the commission, because there was evidently the opportunity of an exhaustive report upon the whole subject, which should have commanded the attention of the country, and would sooner or later have led to some decisive action.

It is plain that so long as we undertake to support the Indians as paupers, and then fail to supply the food; to respect their rights to reservations, and then permit the reservations to be overrun; to give them the best weapons and ammunition, and then furnish the pretext of their using them against us; to treat with them as men, and then hunt them like skunks—so long we shall have the most costly and bloody Indian wars, and the most tragical ambuscades, slaughters, and assassinations. The Indian is undoubtedly a savage, and a savage greatly spoiled by the kind of contact with civilization which he gets at the West. There is generally no interest whatever in him or his fate. But there should be some interest in our own good faith and humanity, in the lives of our soldiers and frontier settlers, and in the taxation to support our Indian policy. All this should certainly be enough to arouse a public demand for a thorough consideration of the subject, and the adoption of a system which should neither be puerile nor disgraceful, and which would tend to spare us the constant repetition of such sorrowful events as the slaughter of Custer and his brave men.

3

A Cavalryman at the Little Bighorn

William O. Taylor

The Battle of the Little Bighorn has been a fascinating subject for historians largely because none of Custer's immediate command lived to recount its details. The only men of the Seventh Cavalry to survive that day were fighting with Major Marcus Reno, whose attack on the Indian village was thrown back just before the "Last Stand" took place. For details of this battle, historians rely on the testimony of Major Reno—given at an inquest at which Reno tried to place himself in the best possible light—and on the published and unpublished accounts of men serving under him.

One of these men was Private William O. Taylor. Taylor served as a "horse handler" during the Reno fight, a soldier who guards the horses when cavalry dismount and fight on foot. Taylor fled the Sioux onslaught with the rest of Reno's command to "Reno Hill," an unsheltered height rising just east of the Little Bighorn. Here, Taylor and the rest of Reno's command dug themselves in. Without water, and running low on ammunition, they fought off Sioux attacks until reinforcements arrived thirty-six hours later. Afterward, Taylor was detailed to help bury the bodies of Custer's men on the battlefield to the north.

Taylor wrote down his experiences in *With Custer on the Little Bighorn*, a memoir he completed in 1917. Not finding a publisher for the work, he donated it to the Memorial Hall Museum at Deerfield, Massachusetts. After his death in 1923 at the age of sixty-eight, the manuscript remained in a black tin box, along with Taylor's western souvenirs—photos, newspaper clippings, and Indian relics.

The manuscript came to light in 1994 after a sale of Custer

memorabilia by a San Francisco auction house. Shuffling through the pages, the buyer, Greg Martin, realized he had uncovered a rare and valuable artifact of the Battle of the Little Bighorn: a firsthand account by a member of the Seventh Cavalry that had never been published and was unknown to historians. Taylor's book was finally published in 1996, 120 years after the battle it describes. The following extract begins in the afternoon of July 25, 1876, as Major Reno leads Taylor and the rest of his command across the clear, cold waters of the Little Bighorn River and into battle.

Major Reno's Battalion, following the Indian trail, marched down a valley through which ran what has since been called Benteen's, or Sundance Creek. This creek flowed into the Little Bighorn river, when there was any water in it, but at this time it was dry. On our way we passed a funeral tepee, which contained the body of a warrior. The tepee had been set on fire by some of our Indian scouts. Afterwards it was learned that the dead warrior was a brother of Circling Bear [Old She Bear] and had been killed in the battle with Crook on the Rosebud, June 17th, eight days before. It has been stated that "a few Indians were seen near here," and that they kept far enough in advance to be out of danger. As to that I can not say, personally I did not see any of them. Then, within a short distance of the river, Reno received an order that caused us to increase our speed and we soon came to the Little Bighorn, a stream some fifty to seventy feet wide, and from two to four feet deep of clear, icy cold water.

Into it our horses plunged without any urging, their thirst was great and also their riders. While waiting for them to drink I took off my hat and, shaping the brim into a scoop, leaned over, filled it and drank the last drop of water I was to have for over twenty-four long hours. The horses having been watered, we rode out of the river and through the underbrush and then a few yards on the prairie, where we dismounted and tightened our saddle girths, and in about ten minutes were heading down a long but rather narrow valley.

On our right was the heavily wooded and very irregular course of the river, flanked by high bluffs. On our left were low foothills near which we could see a part of the [Sioux] pony herds, and as we came nearer, could distinguish mounted men riding in every direction, some in circles, others passing back and forth. They were gathering up their ponies and also making signals. We were then at a fast walk. Soon the command was given to "trot." Then as little puffs of smoke were seen and the "Ping" of bullets spoke out plainly, we were ordered to charge.

Some of the men began to cheer in reply to the Indians' war whoops when Major Reno shouted out, "Stop that noise," and once more there came the command, "Charge!" "Charrrge!" was the way it sounded to me, and it came in such a tone that I turned my head and glanced backward.

The Major and Lieutenant [Benjamin] Hodgson were riding side by side a short distance in the rear of my Company. As I looked back Major Reno was just taking a bottle from his lips. He then passed it to Lieutenant Hodgson. It appeared to be a quart flask, and about one-half or two-thirds full of an amber colored liquid. There was nothing strange about this, and yet the circumstances remained indelibly fixed in my memory. I turned my head to the front as there were other things to claim my attention. What that flask contained, and effect its contents has, is not for me to say, but I have ever since had a very decided belief.

Approaching the Indian Village

In the "Count Off" that morning I was number four, hence when the Troops were dismounted, to fight on foot, every fourth man had three led horses to care for. The position at that time was not to me a desirable one as I wanted to be in the fight, and I had tried in vain to exchange places with my number three man. I have since thought that it was very fortunate perhaps that I did not succeed, for this man, Cornelius Crowley by name, had lately been showing signs of mental eccentricity, or in other words seemed to be losing his mind and the engagement brought matters to a climax in his case. And thereafter he was, so far as possible, kept in charge by the Stable Guard. Had we exchanged places and he had three other excited horses to care for it is a question if he would have been found when we returned to the woods for our horses.

But to resume, the river as I have already said, was a very tortuous one, and at this point it came well out into the prairie, made a sharp turn and then went back to the bluffs.

It was lined on both sides by tall cottonwood trees, and its banks, thick with underbrush so that it shut off the view of the nearest part of the Indian Village which we were fast approaching. Over sage and bullberry bushes, over prickly pears and through a prairie dog village without a thought we rode. A glance along the line shows a lot of set, determined faces, some of them a little pale perhaps, but not altogether with fear. The Death Angel was very near. Was he putting his seal on those who inside of an hour would be lying on the prairie or in the woods, dead, stripped and gashed almost beyond recognition? Be that as it may, there was no flinching on the part of anyone. To most of us it was our first real battle at close range. Our baptism of fire, a new and strange experience, to sit up as a human target, to be shot at and not to return the fire, was a little trying, but our turn was at hand.

"Halt!" came the sharp, quick order, "Prepare to fight on foot," follows at once. Every fourth man from the right remained in his saddle, the others dismounted and tying their horses together, handed the bridle reins to the number four man and sprang forward to their places in the skirmish line. When I look back and think of the sublime audacity of one hundred and fifty Cavalrymen charging with a cheer down on an Indian village that contained at least twenty-five hundred Sioux warriors, and when within close range, dismounting to fight on foot leaving one fourth of their number to hold the horses, it does seem indeed like madness, one hundred fifty men to charge on a village of 1800 lodges.

The led horses, under the charge of Lieutenant [Luther] Hare, were then taken into the woods for greater safety, keeping slightly in rear of the skirmish line. Just how long we remained there I can not say, but I shall never believe that it was over fifteen or twenty minutes at the most. I did not see Major Reno while in the woods nor do I recall hearing any commands as to what we should do. Noise there was aplenty and a few shots went whistling through the underbrush.

Reno and His Troops Retreat

All at once the skirmishers came rushing into the woods seeking their horses which they could not locate at first owing to the underbrush, and a slight change of position. Then I heard someone say, "We must get out of here, quick!"

Number one and two of my set of four saw me and at

once took their horses, leaving me with Con Crowley's horse, and wondering where he was. I soon espied him at a little distance rushing around and shouting, "Where's my horse, Where's my horse?" I yelled at him, perhaps not politely, but effectively, for he hastened toward me. I threw him the bridle-rein and turned my horse in the direction I had seen the men going. All was in the greatest confusion and I dismounted twice and mounted again, all in a few moments, but why, I do not know, unless it was because I saw the others do it and thought they had orders to.

Before I had gone many yards, I looked to my left and rear and saw quite a number of mounted Indians rushing through the woods in the same general direction we were going, as if they were trying to cut off the men who had preceded me. They were so near that my first thought was that they were some of our Indian scouts, but a second look undeceived me. For these Indians were mostly stripped to their fighting costume, a breech-clout at one end, a feather at the other, a whip hanging from their wrist and a gun in their hand. There was one exception however, a sturdy looking chap who was the nearest of all. He wore a magnificent war bonnet of great long feathers encircling his head and hanging down his back, the end trailing along the side of his pony. I did want to take a shot at him but the trees were close together, and I was not a very good marksman. Besides, my comrades seemed bent on getting out of there as soon as possible. So I let him live; I have often wondered since then if that fellow was not one of the "Big Chiefs," Gall, or Black-Moon. However, I continued on my way. The underbrush was very thick and in breaking my way through it my right stirrup was caught and the strap that attached it to the saddle was torn nearly off, so much so that the stirrup was useless and I had to be very careful of my balance. In far less time than it has taken to write this, I emerged from the woods, climbed up a little bank and came out on the prairie a short distance from where we first entered the woods.

The sight that greeted my eyes was certainly very discouraging. Not over two hundred yards away was a large and constantly increasing number of Indian warriors coming toward us as fast as their ponies could travel, a whooping, howling mass of the best horsemen, the most cruel and fiercest fighters in all our country, or any other. They had passed around our left and prevented our return to the ford where we had first crossed the river and now the nearest of them from the opposite side of their ponies were pouring in a most terrific fire.

On my left was a line of comrades headed due east toward the bluffs, which were one half to three-fourths of a mile away and at the base of which flowed the river, its banks at this point being high and precipitous and more or less fringed with a thick growth of underbrush.

The situation was most serious, it was so sudden and incomprehensible. A few moments before, we were "driving the Indians with great ease." [Reno's Report.] Now we were the driven, but there was no time for speculation. Each man ahead of me had his right arm extended firing his revolver at a parallel line of yelling Indians and I at once followed suit. Talk about the "Thin Red Line" of the English. [The "Thin Red Line" is a common expression for English infantry soldiers, who wore red uniform coats.] Here was a thick Red line of Sioux and growing thicker every moment. Out of the clouds of dust, anxious to be in at the death, came hundreds of others, shouting and racing toward the soldiers, most of whom were seeing their first battle, and many, of whom I was one, had never fired a shot from a horse's back.

Riding to Safety

As before stated, my right stirrup was useless and in consequence my seat was not very secure, nor my aim as accurate as it might have been, so I can not say that I did much execution, but I tried to, firing at an Indian directly opposite who I thought was paying special attention to myself. At such a time many thoughts will pass through one's mind with great rapidity. The chances of being wounded or captured were many. One's fate in such a case was easy to imagine, so I reserved one of the six bullets that my revolver contained for the "last resort," myself, but I was not destined to use it in that manner.

A great part of our way lay through a prairie dog village and the numerous holes and mounds made it very unpleasant riding at our rapid gait, for you could not tell what moment your horse might put his foot in a hole and throw you to the ground. A few moments of such riding brought me to what had been, ages ago, the bed of the river. It was some three or four feet lower with a rather abrupt bank down which with a little urging my horse jumped. And as he did so, to steady myself, I reached for the pommel of my saddle with my right hand which still held my revolver. As I did this my revolver fell to the ground, the Indians were crowding in closer, for as they afterwards said "they thought to drive us all into the river and drown us," and I deemed it very unwise to dismount and look for it in the tall grass and weeds. So I hastened along to the river in which I saw a struggling mass of men and horses from whom little streams of blood was coloring the water near them. Lieutenant Hodgson was one of the number and had just been wounded, so I heard him say. I turned my horse a little to the right to avoid the crowd and, jumping him into the river, was soon across.

After a hard struggle I climbed the steep bank, the rapid pace and exertion over the river had completely exhausted my horse and he stood trembling with fatigue and refused to go any further. He was a poor, broken-winded beast at the best, and was to have been condemned long ago but a shortage of mounts made it necessary to take him along. As I was a late comer in that Troop, he was assigned to me, and bore the name of Steamboat, because of the particular noise he made when traveling.

I dismounted and amid whistling of bullets stood there for a few moments waiting for him to get his breath. Then I tried to lead him along but he would not budge a foot. Getting in his rear, I jabbed him with my gun in vain while my comrades were rushing by the bluffs, some mounted, others on foot leading their horses, disappearing over the top. Things looked serious indeed, for to be dismounted in the face of hundreds of Sioux warriors but a short distance away, was like looking into your grave.

In my anger and disgust I gave the beast a parting kick, unslung my carbine and started up the bluff, a mark as I thought for hundreds of rifles, little puffs of dust rising from the ground all around as the bullets buried themselves in the dry dusty hillside. The slope which we were ascending was a funnel shaped ridge, the small end being near the top of the bluff, with narrow, deep ravines on either side terminating within a few yards of the river. It must have been providence that directed us to that particular spot for there was no other place anywhere near that we could have made the ascent with so much haste and so little trouble.

I had gone perhaps one third of the way up when I was

overtaken by a dismounted comrade of my old Troop, [M] named Myers, "Tinker Bill" we used to call him from the fact of his having been a tinner's apprentice before his enlistment. We walked along quite close together for a few feet when with but the single exclamation of "Oh," Myers pitched forward face down to the ground. I bent over him but he was dead, shot between the left ear and eye. It may be my turn next I thought and instead of keeping straight ahead I bore off to the right a little and more into the ravine. Then [I] turned again to the left, zig-zagging as it were but ever going up. Then, within a short distance of the top, I was overtaken by a former comrade of M Troop, Frank Neeley. He was mounted and had a lead horse with him. This horse he turned over to me, very glad to get rid of his charge. It was with a deep feeling of relief that I got into a saddle again for my chances were a little better now, although my new mount was not such a very great improvement over the one I had left behind. This one was called "Old Dutch," and he was all that the name would imply; still I was not "looking in his mouth," he was a horse. So I mounted and rode on over the top of the bluff where I found the greater part of Reno's command. We were soon joined by a few others who barely succeeded in making their escape.

In times past I have wondered how a man felt, when he believed that almost inevitable, sudden death was upon him. I knew it now, for our escape was little less than miraculous when one considers the overwhelming number of Indians and the pitifully disorganized condition in which we made our death-encircled ride in the valley and up the bluffs, pursued by a howling mass of red warriors, naked to the waist, who, maddened and desperate by the terrified cries of their wives and children whose lives were put in jeopardy for the third time within a few weeks, rushed from their camps and, caring nothing for their own lives, were determined to save their families, or die.

They seemed to us, in all their hideousness of paint and feathers, and wild fierce cries, like fiends incarnate, but were they? . . .

Why the Failure?

It has often been asked, if Custer's defeat was not due to Major Reno's failure to push the fight. That is a question about which there is much difference of opinion even among those who were engaged, and it is one that to my mind, is impossible to answer with any degree of certainty.

The ability to anticipate any and every contingency that might arise in a battle with a foe of unknown strength and position is seldom given to mankind. Viewing the matter from afar, and from a military standpoint, with the successful accomplishment of General Custer's plan solely in mind, it is not difficult for some to think that Reno should have stayed in the fight where he began it, regardless of the cost. That Major Reno was not in a proper condition to handle the desperate situation in which he found himself is proved by his own words, as well as the personal observations and statements of several men who were under his command; of this however General Custer was not aware, and neither the officers nor men under Reno felt like saying much about the matter.

In an editorial of the *Northwestern Christian Advocate* of September 7th 1904, under the title "Why General Custer Perished," occurs the following deeply significant statement, "—Major Reno himself told the late Reverend Dr. Arthur Edwards, the editor of the *Northwestern*, and Reno's faithful friend, 'that his strange actions at the battle of the Little Bighorn, were due to the fact that he was drunk.'". . .

Major Reno's Whiskey

"James Coleman and John Smith went up the river on the *Far West* and met the expedition on the Powder River. . . . At that point Coleman was put off for a few days to sell liquor. Canteens, holding three pints were sold for $1.00 a pint. The liquor was brought in 45 gallon barrels and the finer brands (for officers?) were in bottles and packed in casks. When the army moved, the traders followed, going on the boat to the mouth of the Rosebud, where they again sold liquor. Then they went back to the mouth of the Tongue River where Miles City is now and Coleman has lived since. According to Coleman's report the expedition netted them forty thousand dollars from June to December, 1876."

At the Court of Inquiry held at Chicago, November 25th, 1879, Major Reno admitted that he had liquor in his possession at 9 o'clock P.M. on June 25th, but no questions were asked in reference to a time earlier than this. Therefore, under all the circumstances, I have personally no doubt whatever that if Major Reno had maintained his position, either mounted or dismounted, for but a few moments longer, his entire command would have suffered the same fate that befell Custer. For what General Custer, quick witted, clear headed and resourceful could not do with five Companies, it is hard to believe that Reno could do with three, even if that latter had the advantage of a good position.

This conclusion is due to my own knowledge of the very much demoralized condition of our commander, the close proximity to the Indian village of our little force of three small troops, whose position, if we had remained there, would have been unknown to either General Custer or to Captain [Frederick] Benteen, both of whom were several miles away and on the opposite side of a river which was bordered by high and almost impossible bluffs.

That Major Reno should have hesitated to seek out General Custer immediately after his disastrous retreat is not to be wondered at. What acceptable excuse could he offer after such a brief fight in the bottom? No Commander, and General least of all, would be inclined to accept any excuse, for what would have seemed to him, to put it very mildly, as but a half hearted attempt to obey his orders.

Leaving Major Reno's actions out of the case, I feel that overconfidence in himself [Custer], his officers and regiment, together with his underestimating the number of the Indians until it was too late to change his plan of battle, were the two principal causes of his defeat. Had he accepted the offer of the four Troops of the Second Cavalry made him by General [Alfred] Terry, his plan of battle would have undoubtedly been different, and the result likewise.

4

Custer Was Betrayed by Reno and Benteen

Frederick Whittaker

A brevet captain of the Sixth New York Cavalry, Frederick Whittaker was one of many army officers and military men who greatly admired George Armstrong Custer and who were deeply moved by Custer's defeat and death at the Little Bighorn. Shortly after the battle, Whittaker was engaged by Sheldon & Company, a New York publisher, to write a biography of Custer, to include details of Custer's early life, West Point career, Civil War leadership, and Indian fighting.

Whittaker's prejudices in favor of Custer are apparent throughout the book, in which Custer's faults are minimized and his achievements magnified. Whittaker's two principle conclusions on the Battle of the Little Bighorn (given at the end of this selection), however, are instructive to the modern student. They were commonly held in the years following the battle and were used by Custer's wife, Elizabeth Bacon Custer (who willingly collaborated on the book), and Custer's supporters to attack his enemies, excuse his defeat, and defend his reputation.

The book was rapidly written and published, a nineteenth-century precursor to the "instant books" that still appear whenever a newsworthy or scandalous event takes place. The very brief time given to the preparation of this book is apparent in its haphazard structure, overuse of quoted material, repetitious phrasing, and lack of analysis. Yet the passionate stand taken by Whittaker in support of Custer exemplifies the strong feelings the battle raised among the public, which was clamoring for the military to bring the Indian problem to a satisfactory conclusion once and for all. This excerpt begins with a description of Curly, an Indian scout who wandered away from

Excerpted from *A Complete Life of Gen. George A. Custer*, by Frederick Whittaker (New York: Sheldon & Company, 1876).

the battlefield just before the fighting and who was the last surviving member of Custer's command to see him alive.

How [the Little Bighorn] fight went, Curly the Upsaroka scout tells us, he the only man who escaped alive, and who got away to the steamer *Far West* lying at the mouth of the river. His testimony was taken by the officers of [General Alfred] Terry's staff, through an interpreter. It is plain and prosaic in its simplicity, but it tells the tale.

He says he went down with two other Crows and went into action with Custer. The General [Custer's highest brevet (temporary) rank during the Civil War was major general, but at this battle he was a lieutenant colonel], he says, kept down the river on the north bank four miles, after Reno had crossed to the south side above. He thought Reno would drive down the valley, so that they could attack the village on two sides, he believing Reno would take it at the upper end, while he (Custer) would go in at the lower end. Custer had to go farther down the river and farther away from Reno than he wished on account of the steep bank along the north side; but at last he found a ford and dashed for it. The Indians met him and poured in a heavy fire from across the narrow river. Custer dismounted to fight on foot, but could not get his skirmishers over the stream. Meantime hundreds of Indians, on foot and on ponies, poured over the river, which was only about three feet deep, and filled the ravine on each side of Custer's men. Custer then fell back to some high ground behind him and seized the ravines in his immediate vicinity. The Indians completely surrounded Custer and poured in a terrible fire on all sides. They charged Custer on foot in vast numbers, but were again and again driven back. The fight began about 2 o'clock, and lasted, Curly says, almost until the sun went down over the hills. The men fought desperately, and, after the ammunition in their belts was exhausted, went to their saddlebags, got more and continued the fight. He also says the big chief, (Custer) lived until nearly all his men had been killed or wounded, and went about encouraging his soldiers to fight on. Curly says when he saw Custer was hopelessly surrounded, he watched his opportunity, got a Sioux blanket, put it on, and worked up a ravine, and when the Sioux charged he got among them, and they did not know him from one of their own men. There were some mounted Sioux, and seeing one fall, Curly ran to him, mounted his pony, and galloped down as if going towards the white men, but went up a ravine and got away.

When questioned closely by one of the officers, he mentioned one little fact about his escape that is pregnant with light on Custer's fate. When he saw that the party with the General was to be overwhelmed, he went to the General and begged him to let him show him a way to escape. General Custer dropped his head on his breast in thought for a moment, in a way he had of doing. There was a lull in the fight after a charge, the encircling Indians gathering for a fresh attack. In that moment, Custer looked at Curly, waved him away and rode back to the little group of men, to die with them. How many thoughts must have crossed that noble soul in that brief moment. There was no hope of victory if he stayed, nothing but certain death. With the scout he was nearly certain to escape. His horse was a thoroughbred and his way sure. He might have balanced the value of a leader's life against those of his men, and sought his safety. Why did he go back to certain death?

Because he felt that such a death as that which that little band of heroes was about to die, was worth the lives of all the general officers in the world. Thanks to the story of the Crow scout, we know that he had the chance to live alone, and that he deliberately accepted death with his men as the worthier. He weighed, in that brief moment of reflection, all the consequences to America of the lesson of life and the lesson of heroic death, and he chose death. The Indian hovered round the fight, still watching: in the confusion he was not noticed, or taken for a Sioux. He had washed off his Upsaroka paint, and let down his hair like a Sioux. Let us see what he saw.

Curly did not leave Custer until the battle was nearly over, and he describes it as desperate in the extreme. He is quite sure the Indians had more killed than Custer had white men with him.

There was the little group of men on the hill, the Indians hovering round them like hounds baying a lion, dashing up close and receding, the bullets flying like swarms of bees, the men in the little group dropping one by one. At last the charm of Custer's charmed life was broken.

He got a shot in the left side and sat down, with his pistol in his hand. Another shot struck Custer and he fell over. The last officer killed was a man who rode a white horse (believed to be Lieut. [William W.] Cook, Adjutant of the Seventh, as Lieuts. Cook and [James] Calhoun were the only officers who rode white horses, and Lieut. Calhoun was found dead on the skirmish line, near the ford, and probably fell early in the action).

At last they were all gone, every officer of the group. Custer fallen and Cook killed, the remaining men broke. Then the scout fled too.

He says as he rode off he saw, when nearly a mile from the battle-field, a dozen or more soldiers in a ravine, fighting with Sioux all around them. He thinks all were killed, as they were outnumbered five to one, and apparently dismounted. These were no doubt part of the thirty-five missing men reported in the official despatches of General Terry. Curly says he saw one cavalry soldier who had got away. He was well mounted, but shot through both hips, and Curly thinks he died of his wounds, starved to death in the bad lands, or more likely his trail was followed, and he was killed by the Sioux.

Thirty-two men of [George] Yates' company fell with their chief and the other officers on the hill, the rest of them, with Captain Custer's and Captain [Algernon E.] Smith's men, tried to cut their way to the river and all fell in the ravine. . . . Then, says Kill Eagle [Chief of the Blackfeet Sioux], the Indian wounded came streaming back into Sitting Bull's camp, saying: *"We have killed them all: put up your lodges where they are."*

From the account of some Indians who went across the line into British America [Canada], to trade with the Manitoba Indians, we gain more particulars of the last fight than Curly could see. The scout was so utterly broken down with fear and agony of mind when he reached the steamer, that he could not for a long time give a connected account, but his exultant enemies have filled the gap with their boasts. From these it appears that when only a few of the officers were left alive, the Indians made a hand to hand charge, in which Custer fought like a tiger with his sabre when his last shot was gone, that he killed or wounded three Indians with the sabre, and that as he ran the last man through, *Rain-in-the-Face kept his oath and shot Custer.*

While this account disagrees with that of Curly, I am inclined to believe it, for several reasons. Curly was some way off, the confusion was great, and the two brothers Custer were dressed alike and resembled each other closely in figure. I am inclined to believe that it was Colonel Tom Custer whom Curly saw fall as he described it. On the other hand, several Indians who were in the fight have told the same story about the sabre, and have given Big Rain or Rain-in-the-Face, as the man who shot the General. We know Custer to have been a man of great strength and activity, one who had used the sabre freely in the civil war; and in his last struggle such a man would have been as able to kill three Indians. . . . A last reason that is convincing is this. It is well known that the Indians did not mutilate Custer's body, it being the only one in that group entirely spared. The only reason for such a respect could have been a reverence for his valor. It is also well known that the Indians regard the striking of a living enemy *with a hand weapon* as the highest proof of valor possible, placing a very different estimate on shooting an enemy. All the reports of the Indians who reached the British Possessions were unanimous in saying that they dreaded the sabre more than any thing, and this is easily understood when their superstition as to hand weapons is considered. It seems certain that they would never have reverenced Custer's body as they did, had he not struck down their best men in that grim hand-to-hand fight, wherein, among all the brave and strong, he was the bravest and best swordsman of all, the other officers having had but little teaching in the use of the sabre. Be that as it may, it is known that he must have died under circumstances of peculiar heroism to win such respect, and that he was only killed by the bravest Indian of the whole northwest. . . .

The Men Who Fell with Custer

So fell Custer, the brave cavalier, the Christian soldier, surrounded by foes, but dying in harness amid the men he loved. Who fell with him?

There by his side lay his brother Tom, brave Colonel

Custer, a double of the General, who had enlisted as a private soldier at sixteen, was an officer at nineteen, who wore what no other officer in the army could boast of, two medals, each for a flag taken from an enemy in battle. Brave and gentle, courteous and tender, a model officer of cavalry, God be with gallant Tom Custer till the last day. He died like all the Custers, with his face to the sky and his feet to the foe.

Not far off, close together, lay two more of the same family, poor young Boston Custer and little Autie Reed, Custer's nephew, son of that good gentle Christian woman, who had saved Custer himself from a reckless career, whose prayers had helped to make him the Christian knight he became. Brave boys, nearly boys both, no sworn soldier of the state could die more nobly than they, who would not abandon a brother and kinsman. They could do little for him, but they could die with him. Autie was fresh from school a few weeks before, and wild to see the plains with "Uncle Autie" [Custer's nickname]. To take him along it was necessary to give him some official employment, and Custer, knowing that the rough hard life would make a man of the boy, had him and another schoolmate appointed herders, to help drive the great herd of cattle with the column. Rough as the lot was, the lad never complained. He was seeing wild life, which was all he wanted, and had obtained leave to go on this scout with the General. Boston Custer's official position was that of forage master to the Seventh Cavalry, which he had held some time. He had been for years of a consumptive tendency, and his only chance for life was the open air existence of the plains. How far better for him the wild heroic death he died, under the blue sky, fighting like a true Custer, to the slow lingering failing end of a consumptive, which was his certain portion had he lived.

So closed the lives of the three Custers and their young nephew, fallen on that stricken field. It is time to turn to the comrades that fell with them.

The Fallen Comrades

There is something remarkable in the power which Custer apparently possessed of attracting to his side and intimate companionship the noblest and best of the men with whom the army brought him in contact; and the facts of his death bring out this power in a conspicuous manner. It is clear that when he made the division of the regiment into battalions in the morning, Custer knew that heavy work was coming, and intended to take the heaviest work into his own hands, as he always did. Into his own battalion he seems to have gathered all of his own familiar friends, including his three brothers, as knowing he could depend on them to the death. His confidence was well repaid, and we may say today, without fear of contradiction, that Custer and Custer's friends were the flower of the Seventh Cavalry. The battalion that fell with Custer held them nearly all.

There was the Adjutant, Brevet-Colonel Wm. W. Cook, the last officer left living, and whose final fall broke the hearts of his men and ended the battle. Cook was a model of manly beauty, in a very different style from that of Calhoun. Fully as tall (both were over six feet) and as powerfully framed, Cook was the image of a typical English Life Guardsman, with his highbred aristocratic features and long wavy black moustache and whiskers. Like [Captain Miles] Keogh, he was a foreigner, having been born in Canada, whence he entered the American service in the Twenty-fourth New York Cavalry, rising to its colonelcy. The reader has seen his name frequently during Custer's life on the plains. One proud sentence will be his best epitaph. In choosing an officer to command the sharp-shooters of the Seventh Cavalry in the Washita campaign the question was not, says Custer, "to choose a good one, but among many good to choose *the best*." He chose Cook. Let it be written: "Custer said he was his best officer."

By his side was gallant Yates, captain and brevet colonel, tender and true, a man like Calhoun, of old family and gentle blood, who had not hesitated to enter the ranks as a soldier in the war, had enlisted as a boy of sixteen and worked his way up to a captaincy in the Regular Army. Yates was a true, sterling fellow, a soldier to the backbone, with the crack company of the Seventh. They used to call his troop the "band-box troop," so neat were they always, with an affectation of military dandyism. It was a tradition in that company that every man who died from it, "died with his boots on," the homely western phrase that tells such a story of unflinching courage. There fell brave old Yates, game to the last, with every man of the little "band-box troop" in his place, round their leader, who fell with a smile on his lips. He and they had done their duty, and died like men. God will help the widow and fatherless.

The last company commander of all fell near Yates, Lieutenant and Brevet Captain Algernon E. Smith, one more member of that little circle of refined quiet gentlemen who had shared Custer's friendship at Fort Lincoln [in modern-day North Dakota, which served as the Seventh Cavalry's headquarters during the 1876 campaign]. Captain Smith was one of the bravest and most modest of men. One little incident will illustrate his character better than a volume of description. During the civil war, while a captain of volunteers, Captain Smith was detailed on the staff of General Terry, at that desperate storming of Fort Fisher which gave Terry his star in the Regular Army. During the storming, a regiment faltered under the tremendous fire, having lost two color-bearers and all its field officers. Smith seized the colors, led on the regiment, sprang on the parapet, and was among the first in the works, where he fell severely wounded, his left shoulder smashed by a musket ball. For this he was brevetted major of volunteers. The wound healed, but in such a manner that he could never after lift his left arm above the shoulder. He was appointed to the Seventh Cavalry in 1867 and served in every campaign, in familiar intercourse with his brother officers; yet very few in the regiment even knew he had served in the civil war, and none of the ladies would have known that he had been wounded, but for an accidental remark by his wife in 1875, from which it came out that he could not put on his uniform without assistance, on account of his crippled left arm. Algernon Smith died as he had lived, a simple, modest soldier, in front of his men; while behind him lay the twenty-three bodies of the poor disheartened remnant that tried to cut their way out, when all was over and their beloved officer killed.

And now we come to the last of all, the youngest of that little band, Lieutenant William Van W. Reily. His portrait lies before me as these words are written, and it is hard to keep the cold composure of the impartial chronicler as I think of his peculiarly touching history. His father, a gallant officer of the U.S. navy, went down in his ship in the Indian Ocean, and not a soul came back to tell the tale, before Reily was born. That father sailed away from a bride of a few months never to return, and his boy left the mother who idolized him, to meet a similar fate, amid foes as pitiless as the ocean waves. Willie Reily fell next to Custer, and his fair young body was found lying at the feet of his commander. A good, noble-looking face he had, with a certain wistful musing expression, prophetic of his early fate. He had been ill for some time before the expedition started, and the surgeon wished to order him on some post duty, but he refused to stay, and was eager to share the fate of his regiment whatever it might be. He had his dearest wish; he died like his brave father, at his post doing his duty. Let no man say such an end was sad: it was heroic. We must all die some time, but not all like him. To him and all such, America says, "God bless our brave dead."

The Author's Conclusion

I have told the facts of Custer's last battle as closely as the means at hand will permit the truth to be ascertained. Beginning my task with a strong impression, produced by the official reports, that Custer had been rash and imprudent, and that the conduct of [Major Marcus] Reno and [Captain Frederick] Benteen had been that of prudent and brave soldiers, a careful examination of all the accessible evidence has left me no other course than to tell the whole story, to vindicate the reputation of a noble man from unjust aspersions. I leave the facts to the world to judge whether I am not right in these conclusions:—

1. *Had Reno fought as Custer fought, and had Benteen obeyed Custer's orders, the battle of the Little Horn might have proved Custer's last and greatest Indian victory.*

It may be objected to this conclusion that the numbers of the Indians were too great to admit it: but a careful examination of the conflicting statements leads to the belief that these numbers have been exaggerated by Reno in his report, to cover his own conduct. He estimates the Indians at 3,500 "at the least," and the popular impression has since increased this estimate any where up to ten thousand. Herndon, the scout, a much cooler person, puts them at only 2,000 or 2,500; and Benteen thinks they were only 900. One means of approximate computation is unwittingly offered by Reno. Near the close of his report, he mentions the whole village as defiling away before his eyes, and says, "the length of the column was fully equal to that of a large division of the cavalry corps of the Army of the Potomac, as I have seen it on the march." The divisions of the Cavalry Corps, at their strongest, were about 4,000 men; and they had *no women and children with them*. Making the very smallest allowance for led horses, pack horses, squaws and children, it is clear that at least one-half of the column must be taken away to leave the true number of warriors. This would give us 2,000, and if we allow 500 for the losses in fighting Reno and Custer, we come to Herndon's estimate. These numbers were four to one of Custer's, but he had fought such odds before, at the Washita, and come out triumphant. The obstinacy of his attack shows that he expected to conquer. He could have run like Reno had he wished, and Reno says in the report he thought Custer had done so. It is clear, in the light of Custer's previous character, that he held on to the last, expecting to be supported, as he had a right to expect. It was only when he clearly saw he had been betrayed, that he resolved to die game, as it was then too late to retreat.

2. *Had not President [Ulysses S.] Grant, moved by private revenge, displaced Custer from command of the Fort Lincoln column, Custer would be alive to-day and the Indian war settled.* [Grant had agreed to release Custer from his arrest of May 3, 1876 (for leaving Washington without permission), on condition that General Terry take overall command of the Fort Lincoln column to be sent against the Sioux that year.]

The Dakota column would have been confided to the best Indian-fighter of the army; Reno and Benteen would never have dreamed of disobeying their chief, had they not known he was out of favor at court; Custer and [Major General John] Gibbon would have coöperated, as men both familiar with Indian warfare; and cross-purposes would have been avoided.

The action of a court of inquiry, which will be able to call forth the testimony of officers whose names the author withholds from the public at present, will settle whether these conclusions are correct or not. Many witnesses have been deterred from speaking by fear of those superiors whom their evidence will impeach; and these witnesses will be able to swear in public to what they have hitherto only dared to say and write in private. The nation demands such a court, to vindicate the name of a dead hero from the pitiless malignity, which first slew him and then pursued him beyond the grave.

5

I Did My Duty at the Little Bighorn

Marcus Reno

As soon as the first reports of Custer's Last Stand appeared in the nation's newspapers and journals, the public and the press began demanding explanations. Through the summer of 1876, and over the following two years, the pressure grew on the U.S. government to provide that explanation and, if necessary, a scapegoat.

One of Custer's partisans, author Frederick Whittaker, provided much of the pressure by insisting publicly on an official investigation into the actions of Custer and of Custer's subordinate officers, Captain Frederick Benteen and Major Marcus Reno. After the U.S. Congress convened in 1878 and still took no action on the Custer matter, Whittaker wrote directly to President Rutherford B. Hayes. Finally, the administration gave in, and a court of inquiry was convened on January 13, 1879—too late, according to army regulations, for an official court-martial. The inquiry's star witness was Major Marcus Reno.

The following extract of Major Reno's testimony is taken from W.A. Graham's *The Reno Court of Inquiry*, a condensed version of the inquiry's transcript (the questions put to the witnesses are not given). Reno describes his preparations for the attack on the village and defends his decision to retreat across the Little Bighorn and dig in on Reno Hill. He claims not to have heard the firing from downriver that would have indicated another battle, and he denies accusations that he was drunk during the fighting. Although Reno made a strong case for himself, his testimony came under immediate fire from

Excerpted from *The Reno Court of Inquiry: Abstract of the Official Record of Proceedings*, edited by W.A. Graham (Mechanicsburg, PA: Stackpole Books, 1954).

Whittaker and others and is still debated among historians of the battle.

O n the morning of the 25th, Col. Benteen came over to where I was, and while he was there, I discovered that the column was moving. I was not consulted about anything. I never received any direct orders, and exercised the functions of what I imagined were those of a lieutenant colonel. The division into battalions and wings had been annulled before we left the Yellowstone [River], and when the command moved out I followed it. At daylight, after we had marched some distance, the command halted, and I was informed only that the Commanding Officer had gone to the top of the mountain to make observation with regard to the Indians which the scouts had reported to be in sight. He called the officers together and I attended, of course. He said the Indian scouts reported a large village in view from the mountain; that he did not believe it himself, as he had looked with his glass. He then announced that the column would be formed by companies in the order in which they reported ready, and this was done. I continued as before for two or three hours.

About 10 o'clock Lt. [William W.] Cook came to me and said, "The General directs that you take specific command of Companies "M," "A" and "G." I turned and said "Is that all?" He replied "Yes." I made no further inquiry but moved with my column to the second ridge; and between myself and Custer's column was a small ravine which developed into a tributary of the Little Big Horn. I moved parallel to Gen. Custer for some time. Previous to that Capt. Benteen had started to the left up the hill. I had no instruction as to him and asked him where he was going and what he was going to do. His reply was to the effect that he was to drive everything before him on the hill. That was all that passed between us. He had Companies "H," "D" and "K." He went over to the hills and was soon out of sight. The other two columns continued moving on opposite banks of the stream until we came in sight of the tepee that has been referred to, when the Commanding Officer beckoned to me with his hat to cross to the bank where he was. When I got there the battalion was somewhat scattered and I was about opposite the rear of his column. I there received an order from Lt. Cook to move my command to the front. When I got up there, there was a tumult going on among the Indian scouts. They were stripping themselves and preparing to fight. I understood that they had refused to go forward and Gen. Custer had ordered them to give up their guns and horses. I moved forward to the head of the column and shortly after Lt. Cook came to me and said "Gen. Custer directs you to take as rapid a gait as you think prudent and charge the village afterward and you will be supported by the whole outfit."

My Adjutant, Lt. [Benjamin] Hodgson, was on my left and Lt. [George D.] Wallace on his left. He came up and said, laughing, that he was going as volunteer aide. He was not at the time on company duty.

Reno Advances

I took a trot and proceeded to carry out my orders. I crossed the creek and formed my battalion with two companies in line and one in reserve. I had been a good deal in Indian country and was convinced that they were there in overwhelming numbers. I sent back word twice; first, by a man named McIlargy, my striker, to say that the Indians were in front of me in strong force. Receiving no instructions, I sent a second man, Mitchell, a cook. They were the nearest men I could get hold of quick. That was some minutes after and I was convinced that my opinion was correct. I still heard nothing to guide my movement and so proceeded down the valley to carry out my orders.

My first thought was to make my charge with two companies and hold the third as a rallying point, but when I saw the number of Indians I sent my Adjutant to bring the third company on the line. I was in front near the centre and to the right. The Indian scouts had run away, except three or four, and we did not see them again until we got to Powder River, 90 miles away.

We were then at a gallop and I was about 40 paces in advance. I could see a disposition on the part of the Indians to lead us on, and that idea was confirmed when upon advancing a little further I could see them coming out of a ravine in which they had hidden. The ravine was eight or nine hundred yards ahead on what are called the foothills on the left bank. There were also straggling parties of Indians making around to my rear. I saw I could not successfully make

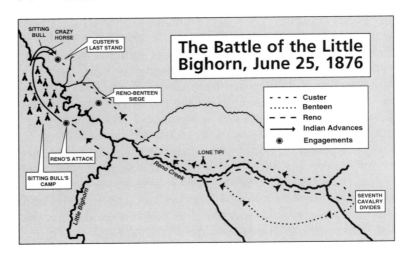

an offensive charge; their numbers had thrown me on the defensive. The village was stretched along the bank to the front and right. There were times going down when I could not see it at all.

I dismounted by giving the order to the company officers. Lt. Hodgson gave it to Company "G" and myself to "M" and "A." I gave the order to dismount and prepare to fight on foot and shelter the horses in the point of timber.

I had an idea of the number of Indians from the trails, and I saw five or six hundred with my own eyes; all the evidences through the bottoms and over the trails showed Indians there. The dust on the trail I followed was four to six inches deep and there were several other trails showing that numbers of animals had gone there.

We were in skirmish line under hot fire for fifteen or twenty minutes. I was on the line near Capt. [Miles] Moylan when word came to me that the Indians were turning my right. I left Lt. Hodgson to bring me word of what went on there and went with Company "G" to the banks of the river. I suppose there were 40 men in the Company. When I got there I had a good view of the tepees and could see many scattering ones. It was plain to me that the Indians were using the woods as much as I was, sheltering themselves and creeping up on me. I then rode out on the plain. Lt. Hodgson came to me and told me they were passing to the left and rear and I told him to bring the line in, round the horses. After going down to the river and seeing the situation, I knew I could not stay there unless I stayed forever.

The regiment [the entire force led by Custer] evidently was scattered, or someone would have brought me an order or aid; and in order to effect a union of the regiment, which I thought absolutely necessary, I moved to the hill where I could be seen, and where I thought I could dispose the men so they could hold out till assistance came. The men had 100 rounds each, 50 in their belts and 50 in the saddle bags; their firing for 20 minutes was what I call quick fire.

Falling Back to Reno Hill

At the time I was in the timber I had not the remotest idea where either the packtrain or Benteen's column were. There was no plan communicated to us; if one existed the subordinate commanders did not know of it.

I left the timber, sending Lt. Hodgson to give the order to Capt. French and giving it in person to Capt. Moylan and Lt. [Donald] McIntosh, to mount their men and bring them to the edge of the timber and form in column of fours. I had no other means of accomplishing the formation.

Where [Custer's scout] Bloody Knife was shot I stood about ten minutes while the formation was going on. I had nothing to do with it. They had their orders to form the men in column of fours out of the timber. I had made up my mind to go through those people and get to the hill for the purpose of getting the regiment together, so as to have a chance to save those who got through. There was no use of staying in the timber when I could assist no one, and create no diversion. I acted on my best judgment and I think events proved me right.

The Indians were increasing, particularly on the right bank, skipping from tree to tree, keeping themselves as much under shelter as possible. They were much more cunning in woodcraft than the soldiers.

The Indians are peculiar in their manner of fighting; they don't go in line or bodies, but in parties of 5 to 40. You see them scattering in all directions. My opinion is that six or seven hundred Indians were there; and I had but 112 men. I thought it my duty to give those men the best chance I could to save themselves; and it was impossible to have a victory over the Indians. I thought it my duty as a military movement, and I took the responsibility.

The column was formed to go through the Indians on that side. I felt sure that some of us would go up; we were bound to; some would get hit and I would lose part of my command. I was willing to risk that in order to save the lives of the others from the desperate position we were in.

I saw Bloody Knife shot, and also a man of "M" Company to whom the attention of the Doctor was at once directed. Bloody Knife was within a few feet of me; I was trying to get from him by signs where the Indians were going. I did not immediately leave the glade and the timber and go on a gallop to the river. I had given orders for the formation and I went through the timber and up on the plain to satisfy myself about the Indians there. Capt. Moylan was at my side. Before Bloody Knife was killed the formation was being made to leave the timber. The column was formed, "A" in front, "M" in rear, and "G" in center. I was at the head of the column and the gait was a rapid one. I thought it my duty to be there, to see about the direction of the column and for observing the ford and the hill on the other side; I would be on the hill to rally and reform the men. I stopped at the river a moment. The men crossed hurriedly and it threw the rear into confusion. They were exposed to heavy fire and I lost many there. The Indians had Winchester rifles and the column made a big target and they were pumping their bullets into it. I did not regard the movement as a triumphant march, nor did I regard it as a retreat. When I reached the hill, after a glance about, I thought it as good a position as I could get in the time I had; and I immediately put the command in skirmish line, through the company commanders.

At the time I left the timber I did not see Benteen's column, nor had I the remotest reason to expect him to unite with me. But in a short time after reaching the hill I saw him not far off and rode out to meet him. I told him what I had done. He moved his battalion to where mine was.

In crossing, Lt. Hodgson, my Adjutant, and a great favorite and friend, had been shot. In the hope that it might be only a wound, and that I might do something for him, I went to the river after Benteen's arrival with some men I called together. Sergeant Culbertson was one of them. I was gone about a half hour. Capt. Benteen was in command while I was gone, and I had complete confidence in him.

He showed me the order from Lt. Cook about bringing up the packs. It was about this effect "Benteen—come on— big village—bring packs" and then a postscript "bring packs," and signed "W.W. Cook." He had not had time to add his official designation as Adjutant. I took a ring and some keys from Lt. Hodgson's body and went back on the hill. The Indians had withdrawn from my front and around me, except for a scattering fire.

Ten wounded had been able to get on the hill with their horses. Most of them men of "A" Company, which led the column. I told Capt. Moylan to make them comfortable and do all that could be done.

The packs were not yet in sight; one of the men was sent after them to get the ammunition mules up as soon as possible. When I had time to look around I told Lt. [Luther] Hare to act as my Adjutant and I sent him to the pack train to hurry it all he could. He went and returned and reported what he had done. In about an hour the packs arrived. I am not positive about the time; I had other things to do than looking at my watch. Before they came up the command was put in position: it was on this hill which I thought would enable everybody to see it, and I kept it there as a nucleus about which the scattered parties could gather, till all came together. That was the purpose for which I went there. . . .

Reno Answers Some Tough Questions

My motive in leaving the timber was, that we had an immense force against us, and nobody came to our assistance. I was not certain that anybody knew where I was, unless directed by the firing. The position, in my judgment, was not tenable, and I thought by placing my command on the hill, the scattered portions of the regiment could get together. It was my opinion that was the only means of getting anybody away alive. The guidon planted by Capt. Benteen on Weir's hill was put there with the thought that it might be discovered by scattered men and detachments.

I heard no firing from down river till after we moved out in that direction and then only a few scattering shots. I thought they were from the village. It did not impress me as coming from a general engagement. Nothing that came to my attention on the 25th or 26th led me to suspect that Custer was destroyed.

My official report was made up in the manner such reports are generally made—from the best information I could obtain. There must have been matters of which I had no personal knowledge as to which I considered my information reliable; especially in regard to time.

I had some whiskey in a flask that I carried in the inside pocket of my uniform sacque; it held about a pint. I did not touch it until about midnight of the 25th. I was not drunk at any time; and the flask was not emptied till the 28th when on the Custer field; it was a most disagreeable sight and officers and men alike were much affected. The stench was sickening. I took one drink on the night of the 25th, but it did not affect me at all. I think it was the only whiskey in the command, except what the Doctor had.

On the 25th I went around the line and came to the packs, and found there a great many skulkers, and drove them out. I did this several times. The horses and mules were safe and I thought these men had no business there. The last time was after the packs had been taken off and I asked one of the men what he was doing there. I was annoyed. I cannot recall his reply, but I know it angered me and I hit him; and I may have told him if I found him there again I would shoot him. This was about 10 P.M., or between 9 and 10.

I never had any intimation that Benteen was to support me in my attack on the bottom. I did not even know where he was.

During the night of the 25th I completed the line by moving some of the companies, and I told all the company commanders to shelter themselves as well as they could, as it would be impossible to leave. I went round the line several times. The Indians that were firing into the herd were able to reach the animals best through the depression, and I tried to fill that up with everything belonging to the packs. I had boxes of ammunition placed along the lines of the different companies, so the men could have all they wanted. Those were about all the orders I gave, and I went around afterward to see that they had been complied with.

On the 26th I moved about, but stayed most of the time with "D" Company near Lt. Wallace. I crossed the ridge several times, and recall being out in front of Benteen's line, and in Moylan's line; in fact, I was around all. After the heaviest firing was over, I was outside Benteen's position with Sgt. DeLacy, to shoot at some Indians we could see galloping around.

I took every means to inform myself that the officers and troops were behaving as well as possible in the circumstances. Frequent orders were not needed; and after the morning of the 26th I did not think any were necessary. I saw no occasion for encouraging either officers or men.

I remained in command after Gen. [Alfred] Terry's arrival, and he sent me to bury the dead, which I thought a proper duty for the 7th—to care for the wounded and bury our comrades, whom we were best able to recognize.

I received no communication from [Fred] Girard at the ford "A"; he had no right to speak to me officially. I had had trouble with Girard, and discharged him because I thought he was stealing from the Government.

My effort to communicate with Custer the night of the 25th was as much for my benefit as for his. I had no more concern, nor as much, about his position as for my own.

There were two Indians, Half Yellow Face and a Crow, who I thought would be able to go through. I would not order a soldier to go to certain death. These Indians talked about it but would not go.

I made an effort on the 26th to communicate with Gen. Terry by a Crow scout. He took the note and left the lines but came back shortly. I do not know what became of the note. I finally got one to Gen. Terry on the 27th.

The only expectation of support I had from the order I received, was from the rear. I do not feel that I failed in my duty and think the results of those two days justify me.

Chapter 2

The Last Stand Through Indian Eyes

1

Cheyenne Warriors Recall the Little Bighorn Battle

George Bird Grinnell

Naturalist George Bird Grinnell, the founder of the Audubon Society, served under Custer as the official naturalist of the Black Hills expedition of 1874. In the following year he joined the Ludlow expedition to Yellowstone. A tireless scholar of the Plains Indians, Grinnell collected a great mass of information and photographs on the Pawnee, Blackfeet, and Cheyenne, including the following interviews with several Cheyenne veterans of the Battle of the Little Bighorn. The interviews were conducted from 1895 through 1908 and, until the publication of *Cheyenne Memories of the Custer Fight* in 1995, were never published.

The descriptions given by Grinnell's subjects reveal that Indians approached warfare in a very different way than did the soldiers of the U.S. Cavalry. Although they were led by war chiefs and charged into battle en masse, they fought as individuals, each seeking out single combat with an adversary. Against other Indians, battles were quite often bloodless, with each warrior striving not to kill but to "count coup," or strike his enemy with his hand or a weapon, and thus gain recognition among his fellow warriors for his bravery. Against the Seventh Cavalry, however, the Cheyenne as well as the Sioux knew they were fighting for their homes, their families, and their way of life. They were in a fight to the death; they strived to kill and they took no prisoners.

In the following selection Grinnell interviews American Horse, a leader of the northern Cheyenne and a member of that tribe's council of chiefs; Brave Wolf; White Bull, a northern Cheyenne shaman who lost his only son in the battle; Soldier Wolf; Tall Bull; White Shield, the grandson of a renowned Cheyenne leader named Whistling Elk; Little Hawk, who also fought against General George Crook at the Battle of the Rosebud; and John Two Moons.

The American Horse Interview

Northern Cheyenne Indian Reservation, Montana, 1895
We first came together and heard that the white soldiers were in the country, down near the mouth of the Rosebud [Creek], close to the Yellowstone [River]. A large camp gathered there. After a while, we all moved up the Rosebud, keeping scouts out all the time. While we were going up the Rosebud, we had a fight with the soldiers [the Battle of Rosebud Creek, which took place on June 17, one week before the Little Bighorn fight]. Afterward we crossed over to Reno Creek and camped. Scouts came in and said that lots of white men (soldiers) were coming.

Next morning we moved on and camped in a big bottom where there is a bunch of timber, the place where we were afterwards attacked [by Custer]. Scouts were kept out all the time. The next day some men were back on the Rosebud, watching to see where the troops with whom they had fought were going. These went the other way, but these scouts discovered Custer going up the Rosebud. A short time after the scout who made this discovery got into camp, four or five lodges of Sioux, who had set out to go to Red Cloud Agency, discovered Custer's troops close to them. These lodges got frightened and turned back, and when they reached the main camp, their report caused great alarm.

Above [on Reno Creek], where the Indians had left the Rosebud, two men, wounded in the first fight on the Rosebud, had died and [had] been left there in lodges. The troops discovered these lodges and charged them, and found not one there alive. The scouts of the Indians saw this.

About this time, the troops turned and went to the head [of the lower forks] and there separated. The next thing I heard [was] an old man haranguing in the camp that the soldiers were about to charge the camp from both ends, the upper and the lower. I was in the Cheyenne camp, at the lower end of the village.

Then everyone who had a horse mounted it, but most of the men were on foot; they had no horses. [Major Marcus] Reno's party was the first to get down to the Indian camp, and most of the men went up there to meet him. I was with those who went to meet Reno, as he was charging down on the flat where the timber stands. When the troops reached this timber, they stopped and went into it, and stopped [again]. The Indians were all around them. Then the Sioux and the Cheyennes charged and the troops ran for the river. The Indians rode right up to them [and] knocked some off their horses as they were running, and some fell off in the river. It was like chasing buffalo—a grand chase.

Reno's troops crossed the river and got up on the hill. Just as the troops got on the hill, the Indians saw a big pack train of mules coming, which met Reno there. The Indians all stopped at the river; they did not try to cross, but turned back to look over the dead for plunder, and to see who of their own people was killed.

While they were doing this, they heard shooting and calling down the river—a man calling out that the troops were attacking the lower end of the village. Then they all rushed down below and saw Custer coming down the hill and almost at the river. I was one of the first to meet the troops and the Indians and the soldiers reached the flat about the same time. When Custer saw them coming, he was down on the river bottom at the river's bank. The troops fought in line of battle, and there they fought for some little time. Then the troops gave way and were driven up the hill. The troops fought on horseback all the way up the hill. They were on their horses as long as the horses lasted, but by this time the Indians had got all around them and they were completely surrounded.

Those [Indians] who were following behind picked up the guns and ammunition belts of the soldiers who had been killed, and [they] fought the troops with their own guns. Many of the belts picked up had no cartridges in them. The soldiers were shooting all the time, as fast as the Indians. There were so many Sioux and Cheyennes that the whole country seemed to be alive with them, closing in on the troops and shooting. They kept following them until they got to a high point, and by this time very few white men were left. Here they closed in on them, and in a moment all were killed. I think this ended about two or three o'clock.

After we had killed those on the hill, we discovered that there were some other white men who had gotten off. They were discovered by people down below, and were below, that is, downstream from the monument. They charged these and killed them all.

After they had finished with Custer, they went back to Reno. It was now pretty late in the afternoon. They had fought there all night and all the next day until the middle of the afternoon. While they were fighting, someone came up the river and reported that troops were coming—a good many. They left Reno and returned to camp, for they had made up their mind that they did not want to fight anymore. They had fought for two days now and thought that they had fought enough. . . .

The Brave Wolf Interview

Northern Cheyenne Indian Reservation, Montana, 1895

I was in the Cheyenne camp, and when Reno made his charge, I went with the rest to meet him. We fought there. I saw the soldiers all go down [into] the timber. I could never understand why they left it, for if they had stayed there, they would have been all right; but they ran out of the timber across the river and up the hill. The citizen packers and the pack mules were on the hill before Reno got there. Then we heard the shooting below, and all rushed down the river.

When I got to the Cheyenne camp, the fighting had been going on for some time. The soldiers (Custer's) were right down close to the stream, but none were on this side. Just as I got there, the soldiers began to retreat up the narrow gulch. They were all drawn up in line of battle, shooting well and fighting hard, but there were so many people around them that they could not help being killed. They still held their line of battle and kept fighting and falling from their horses—fighting and falling all the way up, nearly to where the monument now stands. I think all their horses had been killed before they got quite to the top of the hill. None got there on horseback, and only a few on foot.

A part of those who had reached the top of the hill went on over and tried to go to the stream. But they killed them all going down the hill before any of them got to the creek. It was hard fighting, very hard all the time. I have been in many hard fights, but I never saw such brave men. . . .

The White Bull Interview

Northern Cheyenne Indian Reservation, Montana, 1895

Reno charged the camp from below and got in among the lodges of Sitting Bull's camp, some of which he burned. But Reno got frightened and stopped, and the Indians caught him and he retreated as [stated] in all the accounts. Then word was brought that Custer was coming, and the Indians all began to go back to fight Custer.

Custer rode down to the river bank and formed a line of battle and [prepared] to charge. But then he stopped and fell back up the hill; but he met Indians coming from above and all sides, and again formed a line. It was here that they were killed.

From the men and from the horses of Reno's command, the Indians had obtained many guns and many cartridges which enabled them to fight Custer successfully. If it had not been for this, they could not have killed them so quickly. It was about eleven o'clock when they attacked Reno, and one o'clock when Custer's force had all been killed. The men of Custer's force had not used many of their cartridges. Some had ten cartridges used from their belts and some twenty; but all their saddle pockets were full. . . .

The Soldier Wolf Interview

Northern Cheyenne Indian Reservation, Montana, 1898

I was then seventeen years old, [and] old enough to notice a great many things and to see the reasons for it.

The Cheyennes had been there [on the Little Bighorn] only for one night. Next morning, somewhere about noon, the troops charged down Reno Creek into the upper Sioux village, and drove all the people out and set fire to the lodges. When the people in the lower village heard the shooting up above, they all rushed toward it. Everybody went. The troops retreated and the Indians all rushed in among them. They were all mixed up. The soldiers seemed to be drunk (probably they were panic stricken); they could not shoot at all. The soldiers retreated to the timber and fought behind cover. If they had remained in the timber, the Indians could not have killed them. But all at once—perhaps they got frightened—they rushed out and started to cross the creek. Then it was that the Indians rushed in among them. They crossed the river and went up the high bluff.

When the soldiers got on the ridge, the Indians left

them. When the Indians rushed to meet Reno, all the women and children gathered down at the lower village, and becoming more and more frightened as they listened to the firing, they decided to cross the river to the east side and so to get farther away from the fight. When these women were crossing the river and some were going up the hills, they discovered more troops coming. This was Custer's party. The women ran back and someone rode to where the men were fighting Reno and told them that more soldiers were coming below. Then all the men rushed down the creek again to where the women were.

By this time, Custer had gotten down to the mouth of the dry creek and was on the level flat of the bottom. They began firing and for quite a time fought in the bottom, neither party giving back. There they killed quite a good many horses, and the ground was covered with the horses of the Cheyennes, the Sioux and the white men, and two soldiers were killed and left there. But soon the Indians overpowered the soldiers and they began to give way, retreating slowly, face to the front.

They fell back up the hill until they had come nearly to where the monument now is. Then they turned and rushed over the top of the hill. From this point on, everything was mixed up, for there was a grand charge and nothing clear could be seen for the dust and the people, until all the troops had been killed. Then they ran off the government horses left alive, eighty or ninety head, down into the creek.

After I had gone down with the horses and the fighting was over, the dust cleared away and I looked toward the hill—where the monument is—and saw many Indians still there. I went back to see what they were doing. As I went back, I found lying along the hill, north of the monument, a number of dead soldiers. When I got on the hill, I found that all the soldiers had been killed.

In the fight, only six Cheyennes were killed; some were wounded but not very many. More Sioux were killed and wounded.

Reno's men were frightened and acted as if they were drunk—as I think they were. Custer's men fought well and bravely. . . .

The Tall Bull Interview

Northern Cheyenne Indian Reservation, Montana, 1898
All the troops came down Reno Creek till they reached

a small stream running from the north; there Custer left and went around to the east. Reno went on down to the Little Sheep [Little Bighorn] Creek and crossed and charged into the upper Sioux village. The people all ran out and the troops set the village on fire.

All the lower-village people heard this and rushed up to where the soldiers were. Back of the village that was fired was a high hill, and the Indians all ran up on it and then charged down on the soldiers who retreated into the timber. They did not stop there, but ran right through it and out on the other side. I was present there and tried to cross the river. As the troops were crossing the river, the Indians kept killing them right along.

When the soldiers had all crossed the stream, news came to the Indians from down the creek that more soldiers were coming, and all turned back. They did not pursue the soldiers after they had crossed. All rushed back on the west side of the camp, down to a small dry run that comes in from the east, and there, down close to the river, were the soldiers. The Indians all crossed and they fought there. For quite a long time the troops stood their ground right there. Then they began to back off, fighting all the time, for quite a distance, working up the hill, until they got pretty close to where the monument now is, and then the soldiers turned and rushed to the top of the hill. There they killed them all.

The horses—a good many—all ran down toward the stream northwest, and the people got about them and ran them off. A few soldiers started to run directly down toward Little Sheep Creek, but the Indians killed them all before they got there. The horse I was riding had seven balls in him and dropped dead under me just before I got to the monument. Only six Cheyennes were killed in the fight, but a good many more Sioux [were slain]. . . .

The White Shield Interview

Northern Cheyenne Indian Reservation, Montana, 1908

That morning I went fishing in the Little Bighorn with Black Stone [probably his half brother] and my nephew. My nephew was catching grasshoppers for me. I know nothing about the Reno Fight. The boy sent after grasshoppers came back and said, "An Indian went by wearing a warbonnet—they must be looking for someone." I got on my horse and rode upon a hill and faintly heard much shooting and saw people running to the hills. I knew that the camp had been attacked. I rode into camp. What I had seen from a distance was the Reno Fight.

When I reached camp, all the men were gone, but my mother was leading my war horse around, down in front of the lodge, waiting for me. I bridled my horse and said to my mother, "Where is my war shirt?" She said that a man had just been here who took it to wear in the fight. His name was Bullet Proof. He fixed himself up to fight and tied a [stuffed] kingfisher to his head. . . .

While I was dressing myself and telling my mother which way she should go, I looked back and saw soldiers in seven groups (companies). One company could be seen a long way off [because] the horses were pretty white. I turned to go toward Custer, but some Indians had already seen Custer and were going toward him with others from the camps. I went around and came in below, though the company was coming fast, making for the Little Bighorn. Near me I could see only Roan Bear, Bobtail Horse and one other man. On my side was a man named Mad Wolf who said, "No one should charge yet—the soldiers are too many. Just keep shooting at them."

When the Gray Horse Company got pretty close to the river, they dismounted, and all the soldiers back as far as I could see stopped and dismounted also. When the Gray Horse Company dismounted, the Indians began to fire at them, and the soldiers returned the fire. It was not long before the Indians began to gather in large numbers where I was. After they had been shooting some time, Contrary Big Belly made a charge down in front of the Gray Horse Company and from where the Indians were they saw that the horses of one other company began to get frightened and started to circle around the men who were holding them. When Contrary Big Belly got back, the companies began shooting fast.

I looked across the river and saw two men make a charge on another company, far off to the southeast. These two men were Yellow Nose and my half brother. It was here that Yellow Nose got a company flag, snatching it from the ground where it stood and counted coup with it on [used it to strike] a soldier. When Yellow Nose turned and went back towards the Indians, the horses of the frightened companies broke away from their holders and stampeded, causing someone to cry out, "The soldiers are coming!" The soldiers holding the horses did not let go; they hung on, but the horses got loose anyway.

All the soldiers retreated back from the river; but the Gray Horse Company stood their ground. The Gray Horse Company stood [eventually] where the monument is now. Of the other companies, some left the river, and some went toward it. The Indians charged from all sides and the companies came together a little. By this time three companies ([Algernon E.] Smith, [John J.] Crittenden and [James] Calhoun) had lost their horses, but four still had theirs. One company that lost their horses was near where the road goes now. They were all on foot, going toward the Gray Horse Company. I got around on that side. About half of this company was without guns. They fought with six shooters. It was close fighting, almost hand-to-hand, up that hill. The Gray Horse Company was on foot and kept the Indians off on one side and the other company came across in front of the Gray Horse Company.

Three companies had been killed off before the second three companies and the Gray Horse Company were killed. The three still surviving were half a mile from the Gray Horse Company, toward the hill. Those who survived from the first three companies tried to make their way to the Gray Horse Company, but they did not succeed as all were killed before they got there. Finally, the three surviving companies lost their horses and got up the hill on foot. After the three companies had reached the Gray Horse Company, a man riding a sorrel horse [escaped].

The Gray Horse Company held their horses to the last, and almost all these horses were killed. When the four companies got together, they did not last long. About when the last man dropped in the Gray Horse Company, the Indians made a charge and killed all the wounded with hatchets, arrows, knives etc. Old Bear and Kills in the Night, still living in 1915, chased the man on the sorrel horse, and Old Bear, I think, killed him. The Sioux fired a shot at this soldier but missed. Old Bear then fired, and a little later the soldier fell off his horse, and when they got to him they found he was shot in the back between the shoulders.

Custer was on the outer edge of the Gray Horse Company, toward the river. I saw the man supposed to be Custer being stripped. He was clad in a buckskin shirt—fringed on the breast—and trousers. He wore fine high boots, and had a knife stuck in a scabbard in his boot, and [wore] a big red handkerchief. Lying near him was a six shooter and sabre. He must have died with the pistol in his hand. They had sabers with them. A man supposed to be Custer had a long mustache, but no other hair on his face. He had marks pricked into his skin on the arms above the wrist. This was probably [Capt. Thomas W.] Custer. The Indians did not charge into the soldiers, but shot them from behind the hills. White Bull's son, Mad Wolf or Limber Bones, charged among the soldiers and was killed. . . .

The Little Hawk Interview
Northern Cheyenne Indian Reservation, 1908

The first charge was made by troops who went down Reno Creek and crossed the Little Horn. [They] went down the Little Horn about two miles and halted and went down into a low place where water used to stand and where there is timber among the lodges of one of the villages. The Cheyennes charged him [Reno] and he did not stand but charged through them, going back the way he had come. He did not cross where he had come [from], but jumped over a bank. When he crossed, the Cheyennes did not follow him, for looking back they saw another lot of soldiers coming, and they went back to meet them. Little Hawk went back towards Custer. He does not know what became of Reno.

Little Hawk went back toward Custer and rode up the little ravine which the Indians went up in approaching Custer. The first thing he saw was Chief Comes in Sight on a bobtail horse, riding up and down in front of the soldiers who were firing at him. Contrary Belly and Yellow Nose made the first charge. The two rode part way toward the soldiers and turned their horses and came back. The soldiers were all dismounted to fight on foot. As these two came back, an officer was killed and fell from his horse, and then all the soldiers mounted.

Yellow Nose and Contrary Belly now made a second charge and were followed by the rest of the Indians. When they charged, the soldiers ran and went along the straight ridge where they chased them like buffalo, and as long as they had their backs toward the Indians, the Indians rode right in among them. At the knoll where the monument

[now] stands, the soldiers turned and that is the last place he saw them. White Bull's son and—[illegible] Black fell right in among the soldiers as they were going along. White Bull's son lived till the next day. Twenty-three dead.

Upon this round knoll the soldiers, having tied their horses in fours, let them go and they scattered, most of them running down toward the Little Horn. One company of soldiers went down toward the Little Horn and all but one man dismounted. The man who did not dismount rode away. He was riding a sorrel horse and Indians began to shoot at him, but could not hit him nor overtake him. At last, when he was almost out of shot, a ball hit him and knocked him off his horse. He is the only man who has not a stone [marker].

In the charge up the ridge where soldiers and Indians were together (where White Bull's son and——B[lack] were killed) not many soldiers were slain. Most of them got upon the knoll where the monument now stands. From there the most of them were killed by Indians hidden behind the little ridge, but there was some charging into these troops by Indians. Yellow Nose captured from a soldier a flag which had a gilt lance head on the staff, the only one of this kind taken. About fifteen flags were captured. . . .

The John Two Moons Interview
Northern Cheyenne Indian Reservation, 1908

After the soldiers turned upon the little ridge, the Gray Horse Company stopped where [the present] monument is. The others went on, stopping at intervals until there were four lines, the last opposite to the camp. After they saw soldiers there, [John] Two Moons, who was nearer to the river on a hillside, ran with others and caught their horses and rushed toward the fight. Several charges had been made but no fighting had been done. Indians were struggling up the gulch northeast of the soldiers like ants rushing out of a hill.

Yellow Nose made two dashes toward the soldiers and returned, and said to his people, "Let us charge." The third company—the one toward the river—had moved back a little toward the second. The Indians were trying to drive the three companies on this ridge, running about north and south, over to the Gray Horse Company. Yellow Nose made a third charge, but the other Indians did not follow him.

Meantime, the Indians were getting further to the north,

trying to surround the soldiers. At the fourth charge, on Yellow Nose's orders, all Indians mounted and Yellow Nose made a charge, and all Indians followed. They crowded the company furthest north [south?] and they started to run down the ridge. As they got down part way toward the Gray Horse Company, the latter began to fire and drove the Indians off, and the soldiers reached the Gray Horse Company.

Some [soldiers] were killed, however, when they reached the Gray Horse [Company]. The latter shot at the Indians so fast that they drove the Indians back out of sight over the hill toward the [location of the present Crow] agency. The same Indians called out very loud, "All dismount," and they did so. It was done quickly. When the Indians dismounted, they shot at soldiers who retreated for the top of the hill. Then the Indians mounted and charged. Then the Gray Horse Company turned their horses loose, and some of the horses rushed through the Indians and toward the river.

When the Indians charged to the top of the hill, they saw the other two companies way down near to the river. Then all the soldiers turned their horses loose. The Gray Horse Company was destroyed on the hill near where they went out of sight. The Indians charged in among them. One of the companies retreated down toward a little gulch where they tried to fight under cover. Here the last of the soldiers were killed. He saw and heard what the Gray Horse Company did, and [what] those [did] who took refuge in the little creek. Those in the creek were all killed before he got there.

If these soldiers had all stood together, the Indians could have done nothing with them. The yelling of the Indians seemed to frighten the cavalry horses and they were naying and—[plunging?] so that the men could not handle their guns. If the horses, after they had been turned loose, had come to a shallow place in the Little Horn River, they would have crossed it and no one knows when they would have stopped. [However,] they struck a deep hole in the river and could not get out on the other side, and stayed there swimming around.

2

The Sioux and Cheyenne Won Through Superior Leadership

James Welch

In 1992 James Welch, a novelist and member of the Blackfeet Indian tribe, collaborated on a Public Broadcasting System documentary on the Battle of the Little Bighorn. His first non-fiction book, *Killing Custer* (excerpted here), was drawn from research and interviews carried out on the battlefield, now the site of a national monument. Welch gives a detailed history of the U.S. settlement of the Great Plains from the time of the Lewis and Clark expedition of 1804–1806, describes the encounter of the Blackfeet and the Sioux with the early settlers, and recounts the background of the Sioux campaign of 1876. In his account of the battle, Welch describes in great detail the movements of both Indian warriors and U.S. Cavalry troops at the Little Bighorn.

Welch argues that Custer's own poor decisions were the main cause of his defeat and that Crazy Horse's flanking movement (credited by many authors as the turning point of the battle) came too late to have much effect on the outcome. While describing the battle from the Indian point of view, the author incorporates the latest archaeological and "time-and-motion" studies to re-create the precise movements of Custer and his doomed battalion.

One of the many mysteries which surround the Battle of the Little Bighorn is why the Indians were not better

Excerpted from *Killing Custer: The Battle of the Little Bighorn and the Fate of the Plains Indians*, by James Welch with Paul Stekler (New York: W.W. Norton & Company, 1994). Copyright © 1994 by James Welch and Paul Stekler. Reprinted with permission.

prepared for the 7th Cavalry's attack on their village. Only eight days earlier they had fought off General [George] Crook's thirteen-hundred-man force on the Rosebud [Creek]. They had been told by reservation Indians who were arriving at the big camp daily that there were soldiers to the east. Scouting parties and hunting parties were constantly leaving and returning to camp from all directions. Custer's Crow scouts, about eight miles ahead of Custer's last camp on the morning of [June] 25th, said they could see smoke from the army campfires. If any Sioux or Cheyenne scouts were in the vicinity, they should have seen the smoke too.

And, as a matter of fact, there were Sioux parties in the area that morning. The Crow scouts, on the promontory in the Wolf Mountains known as the Crow's Nest, observed two Sioux riders not far to the west of them, riding right toward them. An attempt was made to ambush these warriors, but the scouts lost sight of them down on the flat. Then they saw a group of six other Sioux hunting buffalo nearby. And another group of four were hunting at the base of the small mountains, not far below the Crow's Nest. There were other sightings of Indians by the Crow scouts, and they became convinced that the enemy had seen the smoke from Custer's camp and were riding back to warn the village. Mitch Boyer, one of Custer's scouts, had seen two Sioux within 150 yards of the camp. He watched them sneak away.

But the final evidence that Custer's command had been discovered came with the news earlier on June 25 that a detachment of soldiers had located a party of Indians on the back trail. One of the packers had lost a box of hardtack on the trail and the squad had been sent to retrieve it. When they arrived at the place where the hardtack had fallen off, they saw a couple of Indian youths breaking open the pack and eating the hardtack. The soldiers fired on them, and one of the Indians, a boy of ten or eleven named Deeds, fell dead, but the other galloped away.

Custer, who had been angry with the Crow and Arikara scouts for suggesting that his command had been discovered, now had to face the fact that the Indians would know within an hour or two not only that he was in the vicinity but precisely where he was. It was at this point that Custer decided he had to attack the village as soon as possible. Normally, army strategy dictated that the best time to attack Indians was at dawn. Large gatherings of Indians usually went to bed after much late-night feasting and dancing and courting and woke up late in the morning. The early-morning attacks had worked at the Washita and Sand Creek, and at the attack on the Blackfeet on the Marias River, and at the Cheyenne village site on the Powder River earlier that year.

Custer had originally planned to lay over under concealment all day on the 25th and attack at dawn on the 26th. If "Custer's Luck" held, the rest of General [Alfred] Terry's Dakota column and General [John] Gibbon's Montana column would arrive at about that time from the west and the Indians would be caught in a loose surround. (Of course, this would require extraordinary luck, and not even Custer would count on it.) But now that he was convinced that his troops had been discovered, all previous plans were thrown to the wind in favor of an immediate attack. As always, in true military mind-set, Custer was afraid that the Indians would escape. This attack would occur, by necessity, at midafternoon, a time when the camp was up and alert and presumably preparing to flee or fight.

Reno's Surprise Attack

So why did [Major Marcus] Reno's charge into the south end of the village where the powerful Hunkpapas had their camp circle come as a surprise? Sitting Bull, the headman of the Hunkpapas and overall chief of the gathering, had been visiting with friends in a council tipi in the center of the camp. Crazy Horse, at the other end of the village, was seeing acquaintances in the Cheyenne circle. Young warriors were fishing or hunting, women were out digging turnips, others were just sitting around, doing sitting chores, waving buffalo-tail fly brushes over napping children, reliving the revelries of the night before. All were in a peaceful mood.

It was customary for Indians to picket their best horses close to their lodges at night to prevent them from being stolen by enemy thieves. But at dawn on the 25th, the horse wranglers drove these horses first to water, then to the large herds on the hills west of camp. So the only horses in the immediate vicinity of the camp belonged to the police, the *akecita*.

Only moments before Reno's attack, the surviving one of the youngsters who had found the hardtack pack rode into camp to tell what happened. At about the same time, an Oglala who was leaving the village to go back to Red Cloud Agency saw a cloud of dust down the valley, then the blue coats of the soldiers. He whirled around and galloped through camp, shouting, "Soldiers coming here! Soldiers coming here!" The women who were digging turnips also hurried into camp, crying out their warning.

The camp became a turmoil of people running, screaming, shouting, gathering weapons. Young men rushed out to the horse herds to gather family horses. Old men yelled advice. Women and children started to run to the hills on the west side of camp. Dogs ran among the lodges, barking. The few horses in the south end of camp grew skittish, making it difficult to mount them.

By now Reno's columns of twos, then fours, had fanned out in full charge position and the sounds of their rifles echoed throughout the camp, bullets striking tipis, buzzing around the Indians "like angry bees," as one would later put it.

The day before, a Cheyenne prophet, Box Elder, had sent a crier around the camp circles, warning the people to keep their horses close to their lodges because the soldiers would come the next day. A Sans Arc had issued the same warning on the 24th. Another Cheyenne had howled like a wolf and a wolf had answered him. That meant fresh meat in camp, dead meat, soldiers. And then there was Sitting Bull's Sun Dance vision—soldiers falling into camp. Then why were the Indians not prepared for this attack?

There have been explanations. The most common is that since the Indians had beaten Crook so badly only eight days before, the Indians did not think the soldiers would be anxious to tangle with them again so soon. Their scouts had watched Crook retreat to the south. They did not know that the eastern column of soldiers was so close (even though they had been warned repeatedly), and they did not know that it was led by Custer, who, unlike many of his contemporaries, would rather fight Indians than eat.

Another explanation that has been offered is that the Indians were in a purely defensive state of mind. They were not looking for a fight, they were looking only to defend their village, and consequently were not as alert or aggressive as they normally would be. It does seem odd that their roving scouts had not picked up smoke from Custer's campsite or seen the dust kicked up by more than six hundred horses and mules. And too, while Custer's troops marched down Ash Creek, they flushed a party of forty Sioux. Fred Gerard, Custer's interpreter, is reported to have said, "Here are your Indians, General, running like the devil." Reno's attack came forty-five minutes later, around 3:00 P.M., surely giving the Sioux party ample time to warn the village and mobilize the warriors. Historian Stephen E. Ambrose thinks that the Lakotas did not see Reno break off from Custer's column and cross the Little Bighorn to attack the south end of the village. They were still tracking Custer's movements.

Although no full explanation has been given for the Indians' lack of preparedness, perhaps a logical speculation would be that the Sioux and Cheyenne leaders knew of the army's penchant for attacking at dawn and had expected the fight to occur the next day. Certainly they didn't expect to be attacked in midafternoon. And perhaps they were just complacent in their strength. Their numbers had been growing by the day and were still growing, almost hourly. In any case, Reno's charge caught the Indians "napping," as Custer is reported to have exclaimed.

But there were a few horses in camp, and a rather cautious counterattack was launched by a few warriors. Although they did not venture too far out from the Hunkpapa camp circle, these warriors managed to break Reno's charge, which could have swept quite a way through the confused village and possibly have given Custer a chance to attack from the northern end and create more confusion. But the faint-hearted Reno ordered his men to dismount and form a skirmish line, a fatal mistake for the overall success of the mission. It should be noted here that even as Reno charged down the valley, he was nervously looking around for Custer's troops, who had disappeared behind the bluffs to the east. On a purely human level, Reno and his troops were shocked when they finally saw the size of the village they were charging. They would have been slaughtered if they had tried to charge into it.

Reno's skirmish line consisted of squads of four—three shooters and one horse holder. The holders took the horses away toward the river, thereby reducing Reno's strength by one-fourth, an incredibly drastic reduction in firepower. But the men were cool at this point and did their job with a fair degree of efficiency.

"Come On. Big Village"

Custer, meanwhile, was heading north behind some tall bluffs on the east side of the river. He was looking for a way down to cross the river and attack the village in its northern reaches. At one halt he galloped over to the top of a high bluff and saw for the first time the huge size of the village. He also saw Reno's 140 troops charging that village. When he rejoined his command he ordered a Sergeant Knipe of Company C to ride back and find the pack train and tell the commanding officer to come quick with extra ammunition packs. Then he moved farther north before riding to the crest of another bluff to view the action. What he saw was Reno's dismounted troops holding their own for the moment at their first skirmish line. Again he rejoined his troops and ordered a trumpeter, Giovanni Martini,* to ride back with a message. Custer's adjutant, W.W. Cooke, not trusting the Italian immigrant's command of English, wrote out the order: "Benteen. Come on. Big Village. Be quick, Bring packs. P.S. Bring Pack. W.W. Cooke." Again Custer rode north, desperately concerned with the overwhelming numbers of Indians but somewhat reassured that Reno was keeping them occupied for the time being. Custer still had visions of a northern assault which would confuse and panic the Indians. At this point, Custer was still on the offensive. . . .

Custer did not know that Reno [had been thrown back and] had been thoroughly discouraged and that Captain [Frederick] Benteen, having gotten the message from trumpeter Martini to "Come on. . . . Bring packs," disobeyed orders by stopping to help the wild-eyed Reno. Custer's five companies would have to go it alone. And now they were split into two separate fighting units. [According to archaeological evidence and the testimony of Sioux and Cheyenne warriors, Custer divided his battalion by sending companies E and F down to the Little Bighorn, for a feint attack, while bringing companies C, I, and L along the bluffs for an attack on the village from the north.]

Custer, who had always relied on "Custer's Luck" in his previous hell-for-leather battles in the Civil War and on the frontier, had done everything wrong in this particular engagement with the Indians. He had not scouted the village

---

*Editor's note: In many accounts, the name of this Italian-American trumpeter is anglicized to John Martin.

or the terrain. He had seriously underestimated the Indians' strength and resolve. He had not listened to his scouts, who had pointed out time and again that the village was immense. He had divided and weakened his forces at every point along the attack route.

As the Cheyenne defenders fired from clumps of brush on the village side of the river, moving and yelling to create the impression there were a large number of Indians, companies E and F moved away to the north, almost leisurely, to high ground on the northwest side of Deep Coulee. Only one trooper, whose horse had bolted across the river, was missing. It has been reported that four mounted Cheyennes, three of them identified as Bobtail Horse, Roan Bear, and Buffalo Calf, crossed the river to harass the soldiers. Custer's battalion on Luce Ridge and Nye-Cartwright Ridge poured heavy fire on the four warriors and on those others across the ford. At this point, both [George] Yates and Custer felt they had time to organize a defensive posture and await reinforcements. But suddenly, hundreds of warriors, led by Gall, arrived from the Reno fight, splashed across the river, and pursued Yates's companies [E and F]. Some rode up Deep Coulee on his right flank. Others crossed farther downstream to attack his left flank.

Caught in the crossfire, and with Indians shooting from the ford, Yates had nowhere to go but up to Calhoun Hill, where Custer's battalion awaited him. Yates set out skirmish lines while he and his troops labored up the hill, with Indian sharpshooters all around them, to reach the reunion point. Casualties began to mount up.

With so many mounted troops and Indians, the hillsides became thick with dust and smoke from the guns. The noise of the rifles, hoofbeats, whinnying and screaming and shouting echoed across the battlefield. The united battalions threw up a heavy fire, which stopped Gall's forces momentarily, killing and wounding several of them. Many of the Indians had dismounted, leaving their ponies in coulees and ravines, and were on foot now, crawling and darting from sagebrush to yucca to clumps of long grass, always moving uphill. Those on horseback again charged the troops, shooting and yelling, waving robes and blankets to frighten the horses. And most of the horses broke loose from the horse holders and stampeded toward the river, taking the troopers' extra ammunition in their saddlebags. The

Indians prized the big American horses for their stamina and strength and fine lines and welcomed them with open arms. The horses, many of them wounded, welcomed the cool water shimmering beneath the relentless sun.

Crazy Horse had not yet appeared on the field. Most of the fighting with Reno and Custer took place without him. But he was leading a large group of Oglalas and Cheyennes downstream to cross the river and attack from the north. When he did show up a short time later, the troops were done for. They were completely surrounded, most of their horses had been driven off, and they found themselves on a naked ridge, vulnerable from all sides.

It is at this point that the troopers panicked. White Bull, a Cheyenne, said that the white men acted as if they were intoxicated, or "beside themselves," shooting wildly in the air. The Indians on foot were picking them off with guns and bows and arrows. Many of the Sioux and Cheyenne warriors found the bows and arrows more effective than guns. They could shoot the arrows without standing up and exposing themselves to return fire. Kate Bighead, a Cheyenne woman who had crossed the river to sing brave-heart songs for her fighting nephew, observed this tactic: "The Indian could keep himself at all times out of sight when sending arrows. Each arrow was shot far upward and forward, not at any soldier in particular, but to curve down and fall where they were. Bullets would not do any harm if shot in that way. But a rain of arrows from thousands of Indian bows, and kept up for a long time, would hit many soldiers and their horses by falling and sticking into their heads or their backs."

Under such heavy pressure, the companies began to break up, some running here, others running there, but always in a pattern of disorganized retreat to the north, then to the west. Now the mounted warriors closed in and began to ride them down, Gall's forces from the south and west, Crazy Horse's men from the north and east. Although several of the troopers were shot, the Indians, true to warrior tradition, preferred to use clubs and hatchets whenever possible, riding close and counting coup [striking their enemies] in a fairly heavy-handed way. One of the Sioux warriors said, "It was just like hunting buffalo."

At least one modern-day authority agrees with this assessment of the troopers' behavior. Richard Fox, an archaeologist who holds a Ph.D. from the University of Calgary and teaches at the University of South Dakota, has come up with a theory which disputes a widely held belief that Custer's troopers fought a controlled action against the Indians, even up to the point of their deaths. According to many historians and buffs, they set up skirmish lines, retreated in order, obeyed their officers' commands, conducted the best fight possible under the circumstances. Their actions are often favorably compared to those of Reno's troops, who retreated from the valley fight in wild disarray and generally just tried to save their own skins. And, of course, the two leaders are compared: Reno was a coward and a drunk, a poor leader who panicked in the valley fight; Custer, on the other hand, was credited with being a strong leader who inspired his men with his derring-do and who fought a strong tactical fight.

According to Fox, however, Custer's troops panicked almost immediately when the Indians attacked in force. They bunched together in helpless clusters, shooting wildly in all directions until their guns were empty. Then many of them took off running, making it easy for the horseback Indians to pursue and kill them. Others stayed in their bunches and allowed themselves to be killed. In fact, Fox uses the term "bunching" to describe this very human, pitiable reaction to a killing force.

It is difficult to argue with Fox's conclusion. In August 1983, a grassfire swept upslope from Deep Ravine near the Little Bighorn and quickly consumed most of the Custer battlefield site. Although this fire was considered something of a (natural) disaster at the time, it turned out to be of enormous benefit to Fox and a team of archaeologists and volunteers. The site, suddenly denuded of knee-high grass, yucca, and sagebrush, offered a clean slate on which to study the battle through the distribution and locations of artifacts. Using a grid system, metal detectors, and controlled excavation, Fox and his volunteers were able to track the development and conclusion of the battle, including tracing shell and bullet patterns as the fight progressed. For instance, he traces shot patterns from where he found large concentrations of shell casings to where he found large concentrations of bullets that matched the shell casings, thereby establishing the locations of the shooters and their targets. Since the cavalry used only two weapons, the .45 caliber Springfield single-shot carbine and the .45 caliber Colt single-action six-shot pistol, it was relatively easy to trace the flight lines of their bullets. But the Indians used every type of gun imaginable, from obsolete muzzle-loaders to modern repeating rifles, such as the Winchester Model 1873 and .44 caliber Henry.

Nevertheless, Fox manages to recreate the movements of the battle for the first time through solid archaeological evidence. He concludes that "the battalion disintegrated. Prior to collapse, fighting appears to have been subdued. Disintegration [of order] occurred early and spread to remaining battlefield sectors. The flow was generally from south to north. There was little or no organization and very little resistance during this process." This is not a pretty picture of the famed 7th Cavalry, and Fox's conclusion is bound to be disputed by Custer buffs and historians alike. Myths of heroism, from the Charge of the Light Brigade to Custer's Last Stand, do not die easily.

The Final Minutes of the Battle

While the companies of the southern positions were being overrun, Custer led his regimental headquarters command, which included his brothers, Captain Tom (who had won a Medal of Honor in the Civil War) and Boston (nominally a civilian "scout" who had never been in that country), and his nephew, Autie (a true civilian who had come to watch Custer whip the Indians), and stragglers from other companies to the far north end of Battle Ridge, to Custer Hill.

By now the troops were spread out all along Battle Ridge, most in small pockets. Those troops on Calhoun Hill were the first to fall. Then the Indians simply rode down the nonresisting troops between Calhoun Hill and Custer Hill. The grave markers today (although often erroneously placed) reflect the direction of the battle and the distribution of the dead soldiers.

There are two groups of gravestones that verify that not all the soldiers died on the ridges. One large group of markers stands at the bottom of Custer Hill to the west, indicating that forty-five or more soldiers, most on foot, had left Custer Hill early in the fighting, according to Indian sources, in a mad dash to reach the river, to find cover in the trees and brush. They didn't come close. They stopped, and those few on horses dismounted and formed a very brief skirmish line. This group probably included the remnants of E Company, the famed gray horse company, although by that point in the battle all the horses were mixed up. These troopers then ran into Deep Ravine, a large, steep ravine that empties into the Little Bighorn. There they were slaughtered like sheep in a pen. The scout and interpreter Mitch Boyer was among those killed at this location, which has been dubbed the South Skirmish Line. A smaller group of fourteen widely scattered markers lie a few hundred feet downslope to the west of Custer Hill. According to Indian accounts, fifteen to twenty soldiers broke and ran toward Deep Ravine near the end of the fighting. White Bull, Sitting Bull's nephew, helped kill them. Big Beaver recalled this development and also recalled that there was no movement left on Custer Hill. Custer and his small group of forty officers, soldiers, and civilians were already dead. "Custer's Last Stand" was not the last of the fighting.

One of the most controversial elements of the battle is testified to by Cheyenne informants. Several of them said that many of the soldiers killed themselves or each other. Wooden Leg says of the South Skirmish Line fight: "All around, the Indians began jumping up, running forward, dodging down, jumping up again, down again, all the time going toward the soldiers. Right away, all of the white men went crazy. Instead of shooting us, they turned their guns upon themselves. Almost before we could get to them, every one of them was dead. They killed themselves." At another part of the battlefield, Wooden Leg is disappointed that the skirmish is over: "By the time I got there, all of the soldiers there were dead. The Indians told me that they had killed only a few of those men, that the men had shot each other and shot themselves." Turtle Rib, a Minneconjou Sioux, saw some of the soldiers shoot each other. He also witnessed, along with others, one soldier break away on a fast horse and gallop away from the battle. Turtle Rib was one of those giving chase, and he says the soldier, on his strong American horse, was pulling away when he took out his pistol and shot himself in the head. Foolish Elk, an Oglala, confirms this.

Kate Bighead saw the fight on the South Skirmish Line: "I think there were about 20 Indians to every soldier there. The soldier horses got scared, and all of them broke loose and ran away toward the river. Just then I saw a soldier shoot himself by holding his revolver at his head. Then another one did the same, and another. Right away, all of them began shooting themselves or shooting each other. I saw several different pairs of them fire their guns at the same time and shoot one another in the breast. For a short time the Indians just stayed where they were and looked."

It may be true that some of the soldiers killed themselves or each other in suicide pacts. One of the first things veteran Indian fighters told recruits was to "save the last bullet for yourself" rather than fall into the Indians' hands. But most Indian accounts do not mention suicide. They say that the soldiers panicked and shot wildly into the air until their guns were empty. Then the Indians killed them. But even today, many Cheyenne elders will insist that the soldiers killed themselves and each other. . . .

The Battle's Aftermath

Who did kill Custer? A man named Hawk said he did. Nobody else said he did. Old Cheyennes told Thomas B. Marquis that a Southern Cheyenne named Brave Bear did it, but they were only joking; they had elected Brave Bear as the culprit because the white reporters wanted a name. Of course, there are other names.

Sitting Bull's elder nephew, White Bull, tells how he killed Custer:

> I charged in. A tall, well-built soldier with yellow hair and mustache saw me coming and tried to bluff me, aiming his rifle at me. But when I rushed him, he threw his rifle at me without shooting. . . . We grabbed each other and wrestled there in the dust and smoke. It was like fighting in a fog. . . . I lashed him across the face with my quirt, striking the coup. . . . But the tall soldier fought hard. He was desperate. He hit me with his fists on the jaw and shoulders, then grabbed my long braids with both hands, pulled my face close and tried to bite my nose off. I yelled for help: "Hey, hey, come over and help me!" Bear Lice and Crow Boy heard me calling and came running. These friends tried to hit the soldier. But we were whirling around, back and forth, so that most of their blows hit me. They knocked me dizzy. I yelled as loud as I could to scare my enemy, but he would not let go. Finally I broke free. He drew his pistol. I wrenched it out of his

hand and struck him with it three or four times on the head, knocked him over, shot him in the head and fired at his heart. I took his pistol and cartridge belt.

Stanley Vestal, who offers this account in his book *Sitting Bull: Champion of the Sioux*, takes White Bull at his word.

Although none of the other Indians would say with certainty who killed Custer, Medicine Bear, a Cheyenne, claimed he counted the third coup on the body. He said the first and second coups were counted by Two Moons and Harshay Wolf.

The butchery and mutilation occurred immediately after the battle. Young boys rode among the bodies, shooting arrows into those that still moved. Then the women came, with hatchets, knives, and stone marrow-bone hammers. According to Iron Hawk, a Hunkpapa who was fourteen at the time, the business wasn't all grim: "The women swarmed up the hill and began stripping the soldiers. They were yelling and laughing and singing. I saw something funny. Two fat old women were stripping a soldier, who was wounded and playing dead. When they had him naked, they began to cut something off that he had, and he jumped up and began fighting with the two fat women. He was swinging one of them around, while the other was trying to stab him with her knife. After awhile, another woman rushed up and shoved her knife into him and he died really dead. It was funny to see the naked *wasichu* fighting with the fat women."

Not all had such a good time. Black Elk recalls his father and uncle, in a rage over the death of the uncle's son, butchering a fat *wasichu*, whose "meat looked good to eat, but we did not eat any." Despite the fact of Rain-in-the-Face's vow to eat Tom Custer's heart and Black Elk's description of the fat soldier's meat, the Sioux, Cheyennes, and Arapahos were not cannibals.

But they did mutilate the corpses horribly. Wooden Leg says, "I went with other Cheyennes along the hills northward to the ground where we had killed all the soldiers. Lots of women and boys were there. The boys were going about making coups by stabbing or shooting arrows into the dead men. Some of the bodies had many arrows sticking in them. Many hands and feet had been cut off, and the limbs and bodies and heads had many stabs and slashes. Some of this had been done by the warriors, during and immediately after the battle. More was added, though, by enraged and weeping women relatives of the Sioux and Cheyennes who had been killed. The women used sheath-knives and hatchets."

John Stands in Timber, whose grandparents were at the Little Bighorn when Custer attacked the camp, was a little more circumspect: "I never heard who damaged the bodies up there. I asked many of them, and most said they did not go [from the village to the battleground]. A few said they had seen others doing it. They did scalp some of the soldiers, but I don't think they took the scalps into camp. The ones who had relatives killed at Sand Creek came out and chopped the heads and arms off, and things like that . . . those who had relatives at Sand Creek might have done plenty. . . . But I think many never admitted what they did. At least nobody would tell the details of what was done to those soldiers' bodies."

Black Elk, who later became an Oglala holy man, was not so reticent in summing up the Indians' feelings toward their adversaries: "I was not sorry at all. I was a happy boy. Those *wasichus* had come to kill our mothers and fathers and us, and it was our country. . . . The soldiers were very foolish to do this."

Among the trophies brought into camp was the battered head of an Indian, a head with graying hair. Two young sisters brought it in, swinging it by the hair like a rag doll. The Sioux and Cheyennes normally parted their hair in the middle and braided it, or left it long and flowing, like Crazy Horse. The Crows cut their hair short in front and left it long and ruffed in the back. But this head's hair was in neither of these styles. Of course, the Sioux recognized the style as that of the Corn Eaters, the Arikaras, their hated enemies. But one woman recognized the head. It was the head of Bloody Knife, Custer's favorite scout. It was also the head of the woman's brother; moreover, it was the head of the girls' uncle. The girls were the woman's daughters. Bloody Knife's sister is reported to have said, "Gall has killed him at last!" Custer had sent the Arikara with Reno in the valley charge, and it was Bloody Knife's brains that splattered Reno, causing him to panic and lose control.

Bloody Knife was only half Arikara. He was Hunkpapa on his father's side and had lived with the Hunkpapas into his early teens, at which time his mother left the band to return to her own people. She took Bloody Knife with her and left his sister with her Lakota father. Most of the Lakotas did not like Bloody Knife as a boy. He was beaten by other boys and particularly incurred the wrath of a young Gall, although no one knows why. A couple of accounts of Bloody Knife as a man mention that his lip seemed always curled with disdain and that he ridiculed and scorned the white men. Perhaps he was that way as a boy. Or perhaps he was treated badly because he was half Corn Eater. Custer enjoyed his company, despite the Arikara's contempt for the general's shooting, and awarded Bloody Knife a silver medallion.

While stripping the soldiers, the Indians found many things amazing. One of the most amazing to them was simply the color of Isaiah Dorman's skin. These Indians had never seen a naked black man up close. Another soldier had gold fillings in his teeth. The Indians were puzzled. They had seen lots of gold, but why would a man put it in his teeth, unless it was the man's personal medicine? Black Elk, who wanted a soldier's uniform and was stripping a corpse, was pushed aside by an older warrior. Instead of getting his uniform, Black Elk had to content himself with a round gold object that he put around his neck: "At first it ticked inside, and then it did not any more. I wore it around my neck a long time before I found out what it was and how to make it tick again." Rising Sun, a Cheyenne, found a similar device, but when it quit ticking, he threw it away in disgust.

Another object that interested the Indians was a small, round, flat case with a needle. If held properly, the needle floated and always pointed toward the north. Since the bodies of the dead troopers lay in this direction, many thought the object pointed only toward white men, and therefore that was how they always found each other.

Among the other things the Indians found were knives, guns, bullets, gloves, boots (the Indians cut the tops off the boots and made sturdy bags of them), military insignia, guidons, flags (including Custer's battle flag), rings, coffee, tobacco, binoculars, McClellan saddles (only the old men thought these would be useful), and religious ornamentation, including at least one scapular belonging to Captain Miles Keogh.

The green picture paper found in leather packets did not excite the warriors. They threw it away or gave it to children to play with. They kept the wallets.

3

The Sioux and Cheyenne Perspective on the Battle

Dee Brown

An Arkansas-born writer of histories and novels set on the American frontier, Dee Brown became a best-selling author with his book *Bury My Heart at Wounded Knee*, which was published in 1970. This was one of the first popular histories of the American West told entirely from the Indian perspective, and it helped bring about an important change in the public's attitude toward the nation's frontier history. Criticism for Brown's alleged factual errors was drowned out by high praise for the author's eloquent condemnation of U.S. government policy toward the Indians and for its powerful debunking of the myths of the American frontier. Brown's account of the broken promises and treaties, forced starvation, and massacre committed by the U.S. government turned what had been a heroic story into a tale of genocide.

The Sioux saw Custer's campaign against them as a fight for the sacred Black Hills, which had been ceded to the Indians by treaty but which, by the summer of 1876, was overrun by gold prospectors. For Brown, who quotes heavily from Indian accounts, the Battle of the Little Bighorn provides a moment of Indian triumph in this long series of defeats and betrayals that ended with yet another broken treaty. Brown recounts the experiences of the Sioux and Cheyenne leaders during the battle and the final moments of General Custer himself, whose death was claimed by several different warriors.

For a long time Crazy Horse had been waiting for a chance to test himself in battle with the Bluecoats. In all the years since the Fetterman fight at Fort Phil Kearny [December 21, 1866], he had studied the soldiers and their ways of fighting. Each time he went into the Black Hills to seek visions, he had asked Wakantanka [the Great Spirit of the Sioux] to give him secret powers so that he would know how to lead the Oglalas to victory if the white men ever came again to make war upon his people. Since the time of his youth, Crazy Horse had known that the world men lived in was only a shadow of the real world. To get into the real world, he had to dream, and when he was in the real world everything seemed to float or dance. In this real world his horse danced as if it were wild or crazy, and this was why he called himself Crazy Horse. He had learned that if he dreamed himself into the real world before going into a fight, he could endure anything.

On this day, June 17, 1876, Crazy Horse dreamed himself into the real world, and he showed the Sioux how to do many things they had never done before while fighting the white man's soldiers. When [General George] Crook sent his pony soldiers in mounted charges [during the Battle of the Rosebud], instead of rushing forward into the fire of their carbines, the Sioux faded off to their flanks and struck weak places in their lines. Crazy Horse kept his warriors mounted and always moving from one place to another. By the time the sun was in the top of the sky he had the soldiers all mixed up in three separate fights. The Bluecoats were accustomed to forming skirmish lines and strong fronts, and when Crazy Horse prevented them from fighting like that they were thrown into confusion. By making many darting charges on their swift ponies, the Sioux kept the soldiers apart and always on the defensive. When the Bluecoats' fire grew too hot, the Sioux would draw away, tantalize a few soldiers into pursuit, and then turn on them with a fury.

The Cheyennes also distinguished themselves that day, especially in the dangerous charges. Chief-Comes-in-Sight was the bravest of all, but as he was swinging his horse about after a charge into the soldiers' flank the animal was shot down in front of a Bluecoat infantry line. Suddenly another horse and rider galloped out from the Cheyennes' position and swerved to shield Chief-Comes-in-Sight from the soldiers' fire. In a moment Chief-Comes-in-Sight was up behind the rider. The rescuer was his sister Buffalo-Calf-Road-Woman, who had come along to help with the horse herds. That was why the Cheyennes always remembered this fight as the Battle Where the Girl Saved Her Brother. The white men called it the Battle of the Rosebud.

When the sun went down, the fighting ended. The Indians knew they had given Three Stars [General Crook] a good fight, but they did not know until the next morning that they had whipped him. At first daylight, Sioux and Cheyenne scouts went out along the ridges, and they could see the Bluecoat column retreating far away to the south. General Crook was returning to his base camp on Goose Creek to await reinforcements or a message from [Major General John] Gibbon, [Alfred] Terry, or Custer. The Indians on the Rosebud were too strong for one column of soldiers.

The Village on the Little Bighorn

After the fight on the Rosebud, the chiefs decided to move west to the valley of the Greasy Grass (Little Bighorn). Scouts had come in with reports of great herds of antelope west of there, and they said grass for the horses was plentiful on the nearby benchlands. Soon the camp circles were spread along the west bank of the twisting Greasy Grass for almost three miles. No one knew for certain how many Indians were there, but the number could not have been smaller than ten thousand people, including three or four thousand warriors. "It was a very big village and you could hardly count the tepees," Black Elk said.

Farthest upstream toward the south was the Hunkpapa camp, with the Blackfoot Sioux nearby. The Hunkpapas always camped at the entrance, or at the head end of the circle, which was the meaning of their name. Below them were the Sans Arcs, Minneconjous, Oglalas, and Brulés. At the north end were the Cheyennes.

The time was early in the Moon When the Chokecherries Are Ripe, with days hot enough for boys to swim in the melted snow water of the Greasy Grass. Hunting parties were coming and going in the direction of the Bighorns, where they had found a few buffalo as well as antelope. The women were digging wild turnips out on the prairies. Every night one or more of the tribal circles held dances, and some nights the chiefs met in councils. "The chiefs of the different tribes met together as equals," Wooden Leg said. "There was only one who was considered as being above all the others. This was Sitting Bull. He was recognized as the one old man chief of all the camps combined."

Sitting Bull did not believe the victory on the Rosebud had fulfilled his prophecy of soldiers falling into the Indian camp. Since the retreat of Three Stars, however, no hunting parties had sighted any Bluecoats between the Powder [to the east] and the Bighorn [to the west].

They did not know until the morning of June 24 that Long Hair Custer was prowling along the Rosebud. Next morning scouts reported that the soldiers had crossed the last high ridge between the Rosebud and the Indian camp and were marching toward the Little Bighorn.

The news of Custer's approach came to the Indians in various ways:

"I and four women were a short distance from the camp digging wild turnips," said Red Horse, one of the Sioux council chiefs. "Suddenly one of the women attracted my attention to a cloud of dust rising a short distance from camp. I soon saw that the soldiers were charging the camp. To the camp I and the women ran. When I arrived a person told me to hurry to the council lodge. The soldiers charged so quickly that we could not talk. We came out of the council lodge and talked in all directions. The Sioux mount horses, take guns, and go fight the soldiers. Women and children mount horses and go, meaning to get out of the way."

Major Reno's Attack

Pte-San-Waste-Win, a cousin of Sitting Bull, was one of the young women digging turnips that morning. She said the soldiers were six to eight miles distant when first sighted. "We could see the flashing of their sabers and saw that there were very many soldiers in the party." The soldiers first seen by Pte-San-Waste-Win and other Indians in the middle of the camp were those in Custer's battalion. These Indians were not aware of Major Marcus Reno's surprise attack against the south end of camp until they heard rifle fire from the direction of the Blackfoot Sioux lodges. "Like that the soldiers were upon us. Through the tepee poles their bullets rattled. . . . The women and children cried, fearing they would be killed, but the men, the Hunkpapa and Blackfeet, the Oglala and Minneconjou, mounted their horses and

The Sioux often participated in war dances to call upon their ancestors for help in ridding themselves of the white man.

raced to the Blackfoot tepees. We could still see the soldiers of Long Hair marching along in the distance, and our men, taken by surprise, and from a point whence they had not expected to be attacked, went singing the song of battle into the fight behind the Blackfoot village."

Black Elk, a thirteen-year-old Oglala boy, was swimming with his companions in the Little Bighorn. The sun was straight above and was getting very hot when he heard a crier shouting in the Hunkpapa camp: "The chargers are coming! They are charging! The chargers are coming!" The warning was repeated by an Oglala crier, and Black Elk could hear the cry going from camp to camp northward to the Cheyennes.

Low Dog, an Oglala chief, heard this same warning cry. "I did not believe it. I thought it was a false alarm. I did not think it possible that any white man would attack us, so strong as we were. . . . Although I did not believe it was a true alarm, I lost no time getting ready. When I got my gun and came out of my lodge the attack had begun at the end of the camp where Sitting Bull and the Hunkpapas were."

Iron Thunder was in the Minneconjou camp. "I did not know anything about Reno's attack until his men were so close that the bullets went through the camp, and everything was in confusion. The horses were so frightened we could not catch them."

Crow King, who was in the Hunkpapa camp, said that Reno's pony soldiers commenced firing at about four hundred yards' distance. The Hunkpapas and Blackfoot Sioux retreated slowly on foot to give the women and children time to go to a place of safety. "Other Indians got our horses. By that time we had warriors enough to turn upon the whites."

Near the Cheyenne camp, three miles to the north, Two Moon was watering his horses. "I washed them off with cool water, then took a swim myself. I came back to the camp afoot. When I got near my lodge, I looked up the Little Bighorn toward Sitting Bull's camp. I saw a great dust rising. It looked like a whirlwind. Soon a Sioux horseman came rushing into camp shouting: 'Soldiers come! Plenty white soldiers!'"

Two Moon ordered the Cheyenne warriors to get their horses, and then told the women to take cover away from the tepee village. "I rode swiftly toward Sitting Bull's camp. Then I saw the white soldiers fighting in a line [Reno's men]. Indians covered the flat. They began to drive the soldiers all mixed up—Sioux, then soldiers, then more Sioux, and all shooting. The air was full of smoke and dust. I saw the soldiers fall back and drop into the riverbed like buffalo fleeing."

The war chief who rallied the Indians and turned back Reno's attack was a muscular, full-chested, thirty-six-year-old Hunkpapa named Pizi, or Gall. Gall had grown up in the tribe as an orphan. While still a young man he distinguished himself as a hunter and warrior, and Sitting Bull adopted him as a younger brother. Some years before, while the [U.S. government Indian] commissioners were attempting to persuade the Sioux to take up farming as a part of the treaty of 1868, Gall went to Fort Rice to speak for the Hunkpapas. "We were born naked," he said, "and have been taught to hunt and live on the game. You tell us that we must learn to farm, live in one house, and take on your ways. Suppose the people living beyond the great sea should come and tell you that you must stop farming and kill your cattle, and take your houses and lands, what would you do? Would you not fight them?" In the decade following that speech, nothing changed Gall's opinion of the white man's self-righteous arrogance, and by the summer of 1876 he was generally accepted by the Hunkpapas as Sitting Bull's lieutenant, the war chief of the tribe.

Reno's first onrush caught several women and children in the open, and the cavalry's flying bullets virtually wiped out Gall's family. "It made my heart bad," he told a newspaperman some years later. "After that I killed all my enemies with the hatchet." His description of the tactics used to block Reno was equally terse: "Sitting Bull and I were at the point where Reno attacked. Sitting Bull was big medicine. The women and children were hastily moved downstream. . . . The women and children caught the horses for the bucks to mount them; the bucks mounted and charged back Reno and checked him, and drove him into the timber."

In military terms, Gall turned Reno's flank and forced him into the woods. He then frightened Reno into making a hasty retreat which the Indians quickly turned into a rout. The result made it possible for Gall to divert hundreds of warriors for a frontal attack against Custer's column, while Crazy Horse and Two Moon struck the flank and rear.

Killing General Custer

Meanwhile Pte-San-Waste-Win and the other women had been anxiously watching the Long Hair's soldiers across the river. "I could hear the music of the bugle and could see the column of soldiers turn to the left to march down to the river where the attack was to be made. . . . Soon I saw a number of Cheyennes ride into the river, then some young men of my band, then others, until there were hundreds of warriors in the river and running up into the ravine. When some hundreds had passed the river and gone into the ravine, the others who were left, still a very great number, moved back from the river and waited for the attack. And I knew that the fighting men of the Sioux, many hundreds in number, were hidden in the ravine behind the hill upon which Long Hair was marching, and he would be attacked from both sides."

Kill Eagle, a Blackfoot Sioux chief, later said that the movement of Indians toward Custer's column was "like a hurricane . . . like bees swarming out of a hive." Hump, the Minneconjou comrade of Gall and Crazy Horse during the old Powder River days, said the first massive charge by the Indians caused the long-haired chief and his men to become confused. "The first dash the Indians made my horse was shot from under me and I was wounded—shot above the knee, and the ball came out at the hip, and I fell and lay right there." Crow King, who was with the Hunkpapas, said: "The greater portion of our warriors came together in their front and we rushed our horses on them. At the same time warriors rode out on each side of them and circled around them until they were surrounded." Thirteen-year-old Black Elk, watching from across the river, could see a big dust whirling on the hill, and then horses began coming out of it with empty saddles.

"The smoke of the shooting and the dust of the horses shut out the hill," Pte-San-Waste-Win said, "and the soldiers fired many shots, but the Sioux shot straight and the soldiers fell dead. The women crossed the river after the men of our village, and when we came to the hill there were no soldiers living and Long Hair lay dead among the rest. . . . The blood of the people was hot and their hearts bad, and they took no prisoners that day."

Crow King said that all the soldiers dismounted when the Indians surrounded them. "They tried to hold on to their horses, but as we pressed closer they let go their horses. We crowded them toward our main camp and killed them all. They kept in order and fought like brave warriors as long as they had a man left."

According to Red Horse, toward the end of the fighting with Custer, "these soldiers became foolish, many throwing away their guns and raising their hands, saying, 'Sioux, pity us; take us prisoners.' The Sioux did not take a single soldier prisoner, but killed all of them; none were alive for even a few minutes."

Long after the battle, White Bull of the Minneconjous drew four pictographs showing himself grappling with and killing a soldier identified as Custer. Among others who claimed to have killed Custer were Rain-in-the-Face, Flat Hip, and Brave Bear. Red Horse said that an unidentified Santee warrior killed Custer. Most Indians who told of the battle said they never saw Custer and did not know who killed him. "We did not know till the fight was over that he was the white chief," Low Dog said.

In an interview given in Canada a year after the battle, Sitting Bull said that he never saw Custer, but that other Indians had seen and recognized him just before he was killed. "He did not wear his long hair as he used to wear it," Sitting Bull said. "It was short, but it was the color of the grass when the frost comes. . . . Where the last stand was made, the Long Hair stood like a sheaf of corn with all the ears fallen around him." But Sitting Bull did not say who killed Custer.

An Arapaho warrior who was riding with the Cheyennes said that Custer was killed by several Indians. "He was dressed in buckskin, coat and pants, and was on his hands and knees. He had been shot through the side, and there was blood coming from his mouth. He seemed to be watching the Indians moving around him. Four soldiers were sitting up around him, but they were all badly wounded. All the other soldiers were down. Then the Indians closed in around him, and I did not see any more."

Regardless of who had killed him, the Long Hair who made the Thieves' Road into the Black Hills was dead with all his men. Reno's soldiers, however, reinforced by those of Major Frederick Benteen, were dug in on a hill farther down the river. The Indians surrounded the hill completely and watched the soldiers through the night, and next morning started fighting them again. During the day, scouts sent out by the chiefs came back with warnings of many more soldiers marching in the direction of the Little Bighorn.

After a council it was decided to break camp. The warriors had expended most of their ammunition, and they knew it would be foolish to try to fight so many soldiers with bows and arrows. The women were told to begin packing, and before sunset they started up the valley toward the Bighorn Mountains, the tribes separating along the way and taking different directions.

Chapter 3

The Modern Analysis

1

The Tactics of Custer and Crazy Horse

Stephen E. Ambrose

Best-selling historian Stephen E. Ambrose set out to explain both sides of the Little Bighorn battle in his book *Crazy Horse and Custer*. In the book, Ambrose reveals that the lives of these two warriors carried many eerie parallels and similarities. As men, they were impulsive and often mischievous loners who greatly prized accolades bestowed on them by friends and companions. As military leaders, both were skilled, courageous, and resourceful, and each had the important ability to learn from past experience.

In the following extract, Ambrose describes the migration of the "hostile" (nonreservation) Sioux into the unceded territory of the Powder River region, the last open range remaining to them. He continues with the campaign against the Sioux drawn up by General Terry and his officers while aboard the steamer *Far West* on the Yellowstone River. The extract ends with an account of the days and hours before the Battle of the Little Bighorn, as Crazy Horse gathers the Sioux for a climactic battle and Custer marches through the dry hills and valleys of what is now southeastern Montana. Hungry for glory and overconfident, Custer prepared to charge an Indian village that held ten times the number of warriors under his own command. The victory that he expected would have been the crowning moment of his military career and would have made him a hero to the entire nation.

The Sioux hadn't seen anything like it since the Fort Phil Kearny days almost ten years earlier. The flow of movement had been reversed. After the treaty of 1868 the Sioux—individuals, families, and bands—had been slowly, reluctantly, moving south and east into the agencies [reservation towns where government agents distributed food and goods to the Indians]. So many went that by 1875 the number of hostiles had shrunk from over ten thousand to less than three thousand; meanwhile the population of the agencies doubled and then doubled again, reaching more than ten thousand in 1875. But by February 1876 the tide had turned and by May of that year, its force was almost overwhelming. The agencies lost half or more of their Indian population. Those who stayed behind were old men, women, and children. Spotted Tail and Red Cloud refused to join the hostiles, but Red Cloud's son Jack was one of those who participated in the exodus.

There were almost as many motives for going north as there were Indians making the trek. Some of the agency Sioux made it as a matter of course—they had been wintering on the agencies and spending the summers with the hostiles for years. In 1876, however, many of these Indians left early, moving to the Powder River in February and were joined by others who wanted a chance at some buffalo. This was a direct result of the United States Government Indian policy, which was almost unbelievably stupid. On the one hand, the government had declared war on the Powder River Indians and was preparing a series of expeditions to march against them. On the other hand, the government was bickering over appropriations to feed the agency Sioux so that no food was arriving at the agencies and the people there were starving. They begged their agents for permission to go hunting up by the Yellowstone and the agents gave it; they had no real choice in the matter—if they had said no, the agency Indians would have starved before their eyes.

But most of the Sioux moving north had more in mind than a good hunt. Some wanted a chance to pick up some coup [i.e., battle honors] and horses at the expense of the Crows. Others brought along trading items—white man's goods—to exchange for robes and furs, which commanded relatively high prices at the agencies. Many were just curious, youngsters who wanted to see Sitting Bull, Crazy Horse, and the other famous Sioux for themselves. Some of the young warriors had never been in a fight and wanted to prove themselves—Jack Red Cloud, for example. In his late teens at this time, he had been living on the agency since 1870 and had not been on a war party; there were many other youngsters like him. Older men came along, some with their families, in order to visit relatives they had not seen in years. Some young warriors were mainly concerned with finding a wife among the hostile women, for rumor had it that they were prettier, livelier, and more fun than the agency squaws.

Above and beyond these (and surely other) motives for leaving the agencies, one reason stood out. The Indians were going north to fight the soldiers and to have one last summer of the old wild life. Most of them seem to have held no illusions about the long-term future. The Army certainly made no attempt to hide its preparations for the campaign, which was common gossip among whites at the Red Cloud and Spotted Tail agencies and the agency Indians knew enough about the white man and his power to realize that the end had come: when the Army took possession of the only buffalo range left in the United States, the Sioux would roam no more. It was almost as if the entire Sioux nation (or at least a goodly portion of it) had decided to have one last, great summer before giving in to the whites.

The hostiles played on this sentiment brilliantly. Sitting Bull sent runners to the agencies in February to tell the Indians there to come on north and have a big fight with the whites. There would be a grand Sun Dance, some real old-time buffalo hunts, an enormous get-together (and no race of people enjoyed getting together more than the Sioux), and a good fight against the soldiers, with plenty of coup for everyone. Crazy Horse told the Cheyennes to come join him for a little fighting against the whites.

The appeal was well-nigh irresistible. Crazy Horse's Oglalas and Sitting Bull's Hunkpapas had already joined hands and were camped on the Rosebud Creek, which flowed into the Yellowstone in eastern Montana. Oglalas from Red Cloud's and Brulés from Spotted Tail's agencies swelled their numbers. Then the Cheyennes, who had also been at Red Cloud Agency, came, fifty lodges strong, to camp near Crazy Horse. Some Blackfeet Sioux from western South Dakota rode into camp, enough to have their own circle of lodges. The Sans Arcs were also there with their own circle of lodges. Santees from the Missouri River came, along with some Assiniboines and Arapahoes.

And as the hostile camp increased in size, it became even more of a magnet to other Indians. It was obvious to every Indian in the northwest Plains that the Army was gunning for them, literally, and that any Indian seen anywhere in the unceded Indian territory would be fair game; it didn't take any particular brains to figure out that when you were caught in a situation like that the best place to be was with your comrades. Agency Indians felt the same way. They remembered [the defeats at] Sand Creek [in 1864] and the Washita [in 1868]: a number of them indicated to white friends, before leaving the agencies to join the hostiles, that they could not feel safe even on the reservation, not with all those troops about. Their only safety lay in numbers, and by April the camp of Sitting Bull and Crazy Horse was where the numbers were. . . .

Sitting Bull's Vision

In early June 1876 the camp moved to the Little Bighorn Valley, a favorite resort of the Indians because of its luxuriant grasses and the plentiful buffalo, deer, and elk. But even so favored a place could not support so many people for very long, and after a few days the camp moved back to the Rosebud Valley. There, the Indians held a Sun Dance.

It was a big one, talked about for decades thereafter. All the people, Sioux and Cheyenne, went into one enormous circle. Everything was done in the old way, according to strict and elaborate ritual. Virgins cut the sacred tree; chiefs carried it into the camp circle; braves counted coup upon it. The buffalo skulls were set up, along with the sacred pipes and other paraphernalia. Many men pierced at that dance, undergoing the self-torture so that Wakan Tanka, the All, would smile upon his people. Sitting Bull, his breast already covered with scars from previous Sun Dances, was the sponsor and leader. He sat on the ground with his back to the sacred Sun Dance pole while his adopted brother, Jumping Bull, lifted a small piece of his, Sitting Bull's, skin with an awl and cut it with a sharp knife. Jumping Bull cut fifty pieces of flesh from Sitting Bull's right arm, then fifty more from the left arm.

With blood streaming down both his arms, Sitting Bull then danced around and around the pole, staring constantly at the sun. He danced after the sun had set, through the night and into the next day; for eighteen hours he danced. Then he fainted. When Black Moon revived him by throwing cold water on his face, Sitting Bull's eyes cleared and he spoke to Black Moon in a low voice. His offering had been accepted, his prayers had been heard. He had had a vision.

Black Moon walked into the middle of the circle and called out, "Sitting Bull wishes to announce that he just heard a voice from above saying, 'I give you these because they have no ears.' He looked up and saw soldiers and some Indians on horseback coming down like grasshoppers, with their heads down and their hats falling off. They were falling right into our camp."

Then the people rejoiced. They did not need a holy man to interpret Sitting Bull's vision—clearly it foretold an attack on the camp by the soldiers, who would all be killed by the Indians. Even the most sophisticated agency Indian present at that Sun Dance was impressed by Sitting Bull's performance and made into a believer. Let the soldiers come!

After the dance, the camp moved back to the valley of the Little Bighorn and settled down on Ash Creek. There, on June 16, Cheyenne scouts rode into camp. They reported that General Crook, old "Three Stars," was coming north again, at the head of a one-thousand-man column of white troops, accompanied by 260 Indian allies, mainly Crows and Shoshonis. The hostiles held a council. Some favored moving out of Crook's way; others wanted to start every warrior in the camp moving toward Crook. Crazy Horse rejected both suggestions. He advised leaving half or more of the warriors in camp, to protect the helpless ones and to provide a reserve, while he rode at the head of 1,500 or so warriors to meet and turn back the Crook column. The advice was accepted. Sitting Bull insisted on coming along, although he was still so weak from his Sun Dance ordeal that he could barely sit a horse and needed a man to help him mount and ride. On the afternoon of June 16, the column set off to attack Crook before Crook could attack the camp.

Crook's column was part of a three-pronged offensive that had been under way for a month. From Fort Ellis in Montana Major General John Gibbon was moving east down the Yellowstone River with 450 men, while General Terry was now coming up the Yellowstone from the east with a total force of 2,700 men. Custer rode with Terry, at the head of the twelve troops of the 7th Cavalry. On the march Custer revealed two facets of his many-sided character. In his official capacity he was as tough, as meticulous, and as professional as any general officer could be. He pushed the men hard, but he pushed himself harder. He had the troopers up before dawn and kept them marching until after dark. He held regular inspections, saw to it that his men had the best available equipment and supplies (they were armed with the 1873 model Springfield .45-70s), and generally saw to their welfare while making certain that they were in fighting trim. . . .

By June 10, Terry and Gibbon were in contact at the mouth of the Rosebud. Between them they had covered the upper Yellowstone to the mouth of Rosebud Creek and seen no tracks indicating that the hostiles might have crossed the river, so they were certain that Sitting Bull was somewhere to the south, camping on the Rosebud, the Tongue, the Little Bighorn, the Powder, or the Bighorn. With Crook coming up from the south, they had the Sioux trapped. Now the job was to locate the Indians before they escaped. Terry decided to send Major Reno and half the 7th Cavalry to the south on a scout of the Powder and Tongue valleys. Custer was to move the other half of the regiment back to the mouth of the Tongue, there to await Reno's return.

Custer strongly opposed Reno's making such a scout. He thought it a "wild goose chase," arguing that the hostiles were on the Rosebud or the Little Bighorn. He also thought it dangerous to leave half the regiment behind when a march of a day or two of all twelve troops of the 7th Cavalry would bring them to the Indian camp. Custer feared that the scouting expedition would put the Indians on the alert and make it possible for them to escape. But his real objection was that Reno, not he, would be in command. He evidently had a shouting argument with Terry about it, but Terry would not budge.

While Custer sat at the mouth of the Tongue, he made the last preparations for the battle he soon expected to fight. He was leaving his dogs behind and had officers and men give up their sabers, which were packed in boxes and stored. Custer left the regimental band behind, along with some staff officers and dismounted troopers. On June 16 the shake-down was complete, and Custer waited for Reno to return. That night in camp he finished an article for *Galaxy*. He was about one hundred miles north of Crook, but had no idea where Crook was. Nor did he know that Crazy Horse was marching that night toward Crook. . . .

A Council of War Aboard the *Far West*

The soldiers were coming. On June 20 [three days after the Battle of the Rosebud, in which the Sioux turned back General Crook, who was approaching the Yellowstone River valley from the south], Reno returned from his reconnaissance. Though Terry had ordered him only to go up the Powder, then down the Tongue, he had exceeded his orders upon reaching the Tongue, where he found some Indian trails leading to the west, perhaps indicating that the big hostile camp was on the Little Bighorn. Reno followed the trail cross-country to the Rosebud, then left it to march down that creek back to the Yellowstone, then to the Tongue. Terry was furious. So was Custer, but for different reasons. Terry wrote his sisters that Reno "had done this in positive defiance of my orders not to go to the Rosebud, in the belief that there were Indians on that stream and that he could make a successful attack on them which would cover up his disobedience. . . ." Custer's complaint was that Reno, having cut loose, then lost heart and returned to the main column. He couldn't imagine how any Indian fighter could leave a hot trail, and he chewed Reno out in no uncertain terms. He told [his wife] Libbie he was going to take up the trail where Reno left it, but "I fear that failure to follow up the Indians has imperilled our plans by giving the village an intimation of our presence. Think of the valuable time lost!"

Through his mouthpiece, correspondent [Mark] Kellogg, Custer managed to get his version of the Reno scouting expedition into the eastern press. Kellogg sent a dispatch to Bennett's New York *Herald*, which Bennett gleefully printed a few days before the Democratic Convention met in St. Louis. Speaking of Reno, the *Herald* quoted Custer as saying, "Few officers have ever had so fine an opportunity to make a successful and telling strike, and few have ever so completely failed to improve their opportunity."

The truth was that every senior officer on the three expeditions—Gibbon, Terry, and Custer—wanted a crack at the hostiles for himself. Each was convinced that no force of Indians, no matter how large, could stand up to their fire power. They all knew that this would be the last big Indian fight on the Plains and that the victor would become one of the Great Captains: his tactics would be studied in West Point classrooms and the nation would give him whatever reward he desired. Crook had felt that way. So had Gibbon, who had marched his men well beyond the point of ordinary human endurance in the hope of catching the hostiles and defeating them by himself. In short, the situation was wide open—it was each general for himself and to the victor belonged the spoils.

Terry now moved his command up the Yellowstone and set up base camp at the mouth of the Rosebud, establishing his headquarters on the steamboat *Far West*. There, on June 21, he held a council of war with Gibbon and Custer. The problem they discussed was how to catch the Indians. They estimated the hostile force at between 800 and 1,000 warriors, but Custer thought that figure too low. He felt there would be 1,500 warriors waiting. That was approximately half the actual number in Sitting Bull's camp, but even had Terry, Gibbon, and Custer known that there were in fact 3,000 or more warriors waiting for them, they would have changed nothing. Lonesome Charley Reynolds, as well as Bloody Knife and the Indian scouts, thought there were too many Sioux for the Army to handle, but there was not a single officer who had the slightest doubt about what the outcome would be if any sizable force of cavalry or infantry was able to attack the Indians en masse. . . .

The focus of Gibbon, Terry, and Custer during their war council on the *Far West* was not on how to defeat the enemy, but on how to catch him. Its object, recalled Gibbon, was "to prevent the escape of the Indians, which was the idea pervading the minds of all of us." Scouts had reported smoke in the direction of the Little Bighorn; Reno had seen a trail leading in that direction; everything indicated that the Indians could be caught there (it is necessary to recall that none of the generals on the *Far West* knew where Crook was or what he was doing—a classic example of the disadvantage of a divided command). The plan was that Custer would lead the 7th Cavalry up the Rosebud to its head, thus blocking escape to the east, then cross the divide to the valley of the Little Bighorn. Gibbon, meanwhile, would go back up the Yellowstone a way, ascend the Bighorn River, and enter the Little Bighorn Valley from the

north. Terry decided to accompany Gibbon, probably because Terry was exhausted from the recent marching and
knew that Custer would set a demanding pace. Gibbon's infantry would be easier to keep up with and he could stay on
the *Far West* much of the way. He may also have felt that
Gibbon had the best chance of finding the hostiles. Mark
Kellogg did not. The journalist decided to go with Custer
on the grounds that Custer was most likely to find and de-
stroy the enemy (or had publisher Bennett told his reporter
to stick with Custer no matter what?).

Terry's Orders to Custer

The following morning, June 22, Terry handed Custer a set
of written orders. In some places he was explicit, in others
permissive, thereby laying the basis for endless controversy
about whether Custer disobeyed orders in the ensuing campaign. Terry ordered Custer to "proceed up the Rosebud in
pursuit of the Indians whose trail was discovered by Major
Reno a few days ago. It is, of course, impossible to give you
any definite instructions in regard to this movement, and
were it not impossible to do so, the Department Commander places too much confidence in your zeal, energy and
ability to impose upon you precise orders which might
hamper your action when nearly in contact with the enemy." That made good military sense—Custer was an experienced commander who had demonstrated his ability to
operate successfully when given *carte blanche*. Nor could
Terry anticipate what Custer might encounter, and he
wisely gave Custer freedom of movement.

If Terry had concluded his orders with that opening
paragraph, there would have been no subsequent controversy. But he went on "to indicate to you [Custer] his [Ter-
ry's] own views of what your action should be, and he
desires that you conform to them unless you see sufficient reason for
departing from them." Once again, the phrase "unless you
see sufficient reason for departing from them" gave Custer
carte blanche, but then Terry added "suggestions" that, read in
one way, could be construed as binding orders. Terry wanted
Custer to proceed past the point where the trail crossed the
Rosebud, continue to move south to the headwaters of the
Tongue, and only then turn west toward the Little Bighorn,
"feeling constantly however to your left so as to preclude the
possibility of the escape of the Indians to the south or south-

Despite being outnumbered, Custer charged the Seventh Cavalry into the Little Bighorn. The Sioux wiped out his entire command by sundown.

east by passing around your left flank." Terry also outlined Gibbon's route of march, but nowhere in his orders did he mention co-operation between the two columns.

After the meeting, Custer saw to it that the cavalrymen got ready. Then he dashed off a note to Libbie: "My darling—I have but a few moments to write, as we move at twelve, and I have my hands full of preparations for the scout. . . . Do not be anxious about me. You would be surprised to know how closely I obey your instructions about keeping with the column. I hope to have a good report to send you by the next mail. . . . A success will start us all towards Lincoln. . . .

"I send you an extract from Genl. Terry's official order, knowing how keenly you appreciate words of commendation and confidence in your dear Bo. [Here Custer copied the opening lines of Terry's order.] Your devoted boy Autie."

At noon, June 22, the 7th Cavalry paraded past Terry and Gibbon. As Custer marched away, Gibbon called out to him, "Now, Custer, don't be greedy, but wait for us." Waving his hand gaily, Custer called over his shoulder, "No, I will not." As he rode away, an officer claimed he heard Terry say, "Custer is happy now, off with a roving command of fifteen days. I told him if he found the Indians not to do as Reno did, but if he thought he could whip them to do so."

Custer marched twelve miles up the Rosebud, then made camp. That night, June 22, he called his own council of war for the officers of the 7th. After they settled down, Custer made a speech. "We are now starting on a scout which we all hope will be successful," he began. "I intend to do everything I can to make it both successful and pleasant for everybody. I am certain that if any regiment in the Service can do what is required of us, we can." Success would depend on surprise, and Custer ordered the officers to make certain that no man strayed from the column, that there was no shooting at game, no unnecessary noise, and especially no trumpet calls. He asked for their full co-operation and support.

Lieutenant Edward S. Godfrey, who was present at the meeting and who later became *the* authority on the battle of the Little Bighorn, recorded the aftermath. "This 'talk' of his [Custer's] was considered at the time as something extraordinary for General Custer, for it was not his habit to unbosom himself to his officers. In it he showed concessions and a reliance on others; there was an indefinable something that was *not* Custer. His manner and tone, usually brusque and aggressive, or somewhat curt, was on this occasion conciliating and subdued. There was something akin to an appeal, as if depressed, that made a deep impression on all present. . . . Lieutenant Wallace and myself walked to our bivouac, for some distance in silence, when Wallace remarked: 'Godfrey, I believe General Custer is going to be killed.' 'Why?' I replied, 'what makes you think so?' 'Because,' said he, 'I have never heard Custer talk in that way before.'"

Marching to the Little Bighorn

On June 23 and 24 the column marched up the Rosebud, making nearly sixty miles on the two days. Indian signs were everywhere—the grass was close-cropped for miles around, indicating a huge pony herd; there were burned-out campfires here and there; trails leading west, toward the Little Bighorn; the frame of the deserted Sun Dance lodge. The Sioux had left drawings in the sand that told the story of Sitting Bull's vision, which greatly excited the Indian scouts, but when they fearfully told Custer what it meant, he shrugged.

Late on June 24 the column reached the point on the Rosebud at which the Indians had crossed the stream a few days earlier, headed toward the Little Bighorn. The trail was a mile wide, the whole valley so scratched up by thousands of travois poles that it gave the appearance of a freshly plowed field. Even the dullest trooper knew now that there were "heaps and heaps of Injins" ahead. At 8 P.M. Custer made camp; he was about eighteen miles north of the site of Crook's battle on the Rosebud a week earlier—and he had made thirty miles that day. Here Custer could have rested his men and horses, then moved farther south the next day, in accordance with Terry's suggestion (or was it an order?).

But the enemy was to the west, not the south, and Custer was hardly the soldier to march away from the enemy's known position. He decided to cross over the divide between the Rosebud and the Little Bighorn. He called his officers to him and ordered a night march. This was another inexplicable decision; it further weakened the striking power of an already exhausted 7th Cavalry. Why all the haste? Perhaps the opening date of the Democratic Convention, only three days away, had something to do with it. Kellogg would need time to write his dispatch, take it to the *Far West*, and get the news on the telegraph to St. Louis. It was already the night of June 24–25; Custer needed to fight his battle soon if he wanted to stampede the Democratic Convention. Whatever his reasons, Custer was pushing hard now, the smell of battle in his nostrils.

A night march is, by its very nature, much more difficult and exhausting than the same one made by daylight, but Custer got ten miles out of his men before stopping. At 2 A.M., June 25, he sent Lieutenant Charles A. Varnum and the Crow scouts on ahead to locate the enemy while the men boiled coffee and rested (the scouts were very angry at Custer for allowing the men to make fires). Custer told his officers he would rest the command through the day (June 25), then attack at dawn on June 26, the day Gibbon was expected to arrive on the Little Bighorn.

At first light on June 25 Varnum, Mitch Bouyer (a famous scout lent to Custer by Gibbon), and the Indian scouts were up on Crow's Nest, looking down on the Little Bighorn, fifteen miles distant. As the light strengthened, they saw a sight that made them gasp with astonishment. Intervening bluffs cut off a full view, but the valley was white with lodges, and to the northwest the smoke from the hostile campfires made a murky haze. On the flats beyond the west bank of the river, they could see the greatest pony herd that any of them had ever seen—the pintos covered the earth like a carpet.

When Bloody Knife reported back to Custer, he begged Custer to use extreme caution, declaring that there were more Sioux ahead than the soldiers had bullets, enough Indians to keep the 7th Cavalry busy fighting for two or three days. Custer brushed the warning aside, saying with a smile that he guessed they could do the job in a day. Mitch Bouyer told him that it was the largest encampment ever collected on the northwest Plains and reminded Custer that he, Bouyer, had been in these parts for thirty years. Custer shrugged.

Without finishing his breakfast, Custer, mounted bareback, rode around the camp snapping out orders to his officers. He was wearing a blue-gray flannel shirt, buckskin trousers, long boots, and a regular Army hat over his recently cut hair. He got the column in motion, then rode on ahead to Crow's Nest to see for himself. By the time he arrived, however, a haze had settled over the Little Bighorn and he could see nothing. Custer rode back to the main column. Shortly thereafter, Varnum came in to report that the Indians seemed to be packing up and moving. That was what Custer feared most—that the enemy would get away—and to make matters worse Sioux scouts had been seen riding toward the river. Custer reasoned that they would give the alarm and the Indians would flee. He decided to abandon his plan to rest the men somewhere near the divide, then attack the next morning—instead, he would attack at once.

There was no point to further concealment. He had his bugler sound Officer's Call, the first time a bugle had been blown for two days. Custer informed his officers that "the largest Indian camp on the North American continent is ahead and I am going to attack it." He cautioned them to make certain that each of their men had a full one hundred rounds of ammunition and then he split up the column. Captain Frederick Benteen would take command of three troops, Major Reno another three. One troop would remain with the ammunition train. Custer himself kept five troops.

And away Custer and the 611 men of the 7th Cavalry marched toward the Little Bighorn, where Crazy Horse and 3,000 warriors were waiting. With the difference in weaponry and discipline, the odds were even. This battle would be decided by generalship, not numbers.

2

Custer Could Have Won the Battle

Robert M. Utley

Although not a single member of Custer's command survived to tell the tale of the battle itself, decisions Custer made as he reached the valley of the Little Bighorn on the morning of June 25, 1876, were very well documented in the weeks that followed. In government inquiries, in testimony by Seventh Cavalry officers and enlisted men who survived the battle, in accounts by Custer's own Indian scouts and by the Sioux and Cheyenne warriors who fought him, Custer's plans and expectations can be clearly seen and understood.

Historian Robert M. Utley, a renowned modern historian of the nineteenth-century frontier and the Plains Indians, carefully analyzes these decisions in his book *Cavalier in Buckskin*, excerpted here. Utley concludes that, at their final meeting, Custer's commander, General Alfred Terry, gave Custer free reign to proceed as he saw fit; that Custer was influenced by his past experience in Indian fighting; that Custer's decision to attack on June 25, instead of waiting another day, was sound; and that Custer could have won the battle had Major Marcus Reno and Captain Frederick Benteen not failed him at the last. After giving several possible different outcomes had circumstances been slightly different, Utley concludes, as do many other historians of this battle, that on that hot and dusty day the renowned "Custer Luck" simply ran out.

How could it have happened? What flagrant blunders produced so awful a debacle? How could a commander and a regiment widely perceived as the best on the fron-

Excerpted from *Cavalier in Buckskin: George Armstrong Custer and the Western Military Frontier*, by Robert M. Utley (Norman: University of Oklahoma Press, 1988). Copyright © 1988 by the University of Oklahoma Press. Reprinted with permission.

tier succumb so spectacularly to a mob of untrained, unlettered natives?

The simplest answer, usually overlooked, is that the army lost largely because the Indians won. To ascribe defeat entirely to military failings is to devalue Indian strength and leadership. The Sioux and Cheyennes were strong, confident, united, well led, well armed, outraged by the government's war aims, and ready to fight if pressed. Rarely had the army encountered such a mighty combination in an Indian adversary. Perhaps no strategy or tactics could have prevailed against Sitting Bull's power.

But this explanation exonerates all the military chiefs and yields no scapegoat in blue. George Armstrong Custer is the favored candidate. Driven to win a great victory and wipe out the humiliation[1] inflicted by President [Ulysses S.] Grant, he rushed up the Rosebud [Creek] and plunged into battle before the cooperating units could get in place. He disobeyed [General Alfred] Terry's orders by taking a direct rather than a circuitous route to his destination. He attacked a day early, with an exhausted command and without adequate reconnaissance. Violating an elementary military maxim, he divided his force in the face of a superior enemy and then lost control of all but the element retained under his personal direction, and perhaps, in the end, even of that.

Analysis of this indictment must take account of the character of the evidence on which it rests. No sooner had Custer's body been buried on Custer Hill than all the principals—Terry, [John] Gibbon, [Major James] Brisbin, [Major Marcus] Reno, [Captain Frederick] Benteen—began to recompose the history of recent events. Eager to explain the calamity and avert any culpability of their own, they conveniently forgot some things that had happened and remembered some things that had not happened. Their efforts freighted the historical record with firsthand evidence that threw the blame on Custer and powerfully influenced historical interpretation for generations to come.

This self-serving evidence is not without historical value. But only by rigorously comparing it with evidence

1. During a political scandal in the spring of 1876, President Ulysses S. Grant, a political rival of Custer's, had refused Custer permission to leave Washington, which would have forced Custer to miss the Sioux campaign. When Custer left the capital anyway, Grant ordered him arrested. Later, Grant released Custer under pressure from Philip Sheridan.

dating from before the fatal last hour on Battle Ridge can a true understanding of the dynamics of the disaster be reached. A vital step in such an analysis is to strike out of the equation any facts, however plain now, unknown to Custer then. At each critical decision point the test is what he knew and what he could reasonably be expected to foresee.

In such a comparison and analysis most of the charges against Custer collapse. Undoubtedly he hoped to win a great victory for himself and the Seventh Cavalry. But he did not rush up the Rosebud any faster than had been planned on the [river steamboat] *Far West*. He did not disobey Terry's orders; they were entirely discretionary and, because of the uncertain location of the Indians, could not have been otherwise. He did not precipitate battle a day before Terry intended, for Terry did not and could not fix any day for the attack; Custer's mission was to attack the Indians whenever and wherever he found them. Custer did not take an exhausted regiment into battle; the men were tired, as soldiers in the field usually are, but no more so than normal on campaign.

That Terry intended Custer to use his own judgment in finding and striking the Indians is made abundantly clear by the written orders, by evidence of what occurred in the conference on the *Far West*, and by the simple logic of what was and was not known to the strategists on June 21.

In addition there is the much-debated affidavit of Mary Adams, Custer's black cook. Until recently most students thought this affidavit spurious because they did not believe that Mary Adams accompanied the expedition. Now she is known to have been with Custer. According to the affidavit she executed in 1878, either on the night of June 21 or the next morning Terry came to Custer's bivouac, and she overheard their conversation. "Custer," said Terry, "I do not know what to say for the last." "Say whatever you want to say," replied Custer. "Use your own judgment and do what you think best if you strike the trail," said Terry. "And whatever you do, Custer, hold on to your wounded."

General Custer's Decisions

Custer's first critical decision was to follow the Indian trail over the Rosebud Divide instead of continuing up the Rosebud, as suggested in his orders from Terry. The sudden freshness of the trail on the afternoon of June 24 was all the justification he needed. Plainly, Indians were just over the mountain, a day's march away. His assignment was to find and attack them. The surest and quickest way was to follow the trail.

The fresh Indian sign provided persuasive rationale for what he probably would have done anyway. The judgment to which Terry deferred would likely have kept him on the trail until he overhauled the Indians, wherever they were. A circuit up the Rosebud would have heightened the chances of striking the quarry from the south and driving them toward Gibbon. But it may be doubted that Custer, secure in the conviction that the Seventh alone could handle the enemy, gave much thought to a role for Gibbon or much cared whether he struck from the north or the south. Had the Indians continued their movement up the Little Bighorn, as the chiefs had planned, the attack would indeed have come from the north. Only the chance discovery of antelope herds, prompting the return of the village down the valley, brought Custer in from the south.

The fresh trail also held implications for enemy strength, which Custer failed to note. By the evening of June 24 the Crow and Ree scouts knew that there were more Indians across the Rosebud Divide than anyone suspected. They dropped enough clues that Custer might have taken their worries more seriously and might have questioned them intently in order to bring into the open what they thought and why.

But Custer was not concerned with how many Indians he would encounter, only with preventing their flight. Knowledge of their actual strength would not have changed his dispositions. He had total confidence in the capability of the Seventh Cavalry to whip any number of Indians.

So did all the other generals, from [General Philip] Sheridan down. Most experience with Indian warfare showed that a charge into a village, however large, wrought panic and fleeing Indians, as at the Washita [a battle that took place on November 27, 1868, in what is now western Oklahoma, at which Custer defeated a village of Cheyenne]. But this year the Indians were not only numerous but full of fight, as [General George] Crook had discovered when hundreds of warriors uncharacteristically attacked him in open battle [at the Rosebud on June 17]. News of Crook's defeat on the Rosebud had not reached the Yellowstone, however, and Custer cannot be severely faulted for a mindset shared with his fellow commanders.

It was a mindset, indeed, shared with all his fellow citizens and thus in large part derived from them. That the generals had such contempt for the fighting prowess of their foe as to care little for their numbers was but one symptom of society's attitudes toward Indians. The cultural and racial arrogance of the American people found expression in their generals. Combined with the personal conceit of Custer, this was a deadly mixture. Unquestionably, Custer underestimated his opponents.

Much of what went wrong stemmed from the decision to attack on June 25 instead of the next day, as Custer intended until Sioux were spotted in the vicinity of the command. This decision forced battle before reconnaissance had developed the location of the enemy and the nature of the terrain on which the fight would take place. It prompted Benteen's scout to the left, which would not have been needed had the absence of Indians on the upper Little Bighorn already been established. It led to an afternoon attack rather than the preferred dawn attack. And it decreed a battle plan that had to unfold as information and circumstances unfolded, rather than one conceived in advance.

Despite the consequences, the decision to attack on June 25 was sound. Custer had ample reason to suppose himself discovered and to expect that the village would bolt as soon as alerted. This did not happen because the Indians who observed him continued eastward toward the agencies or were on the way from the agencies to the village. That afternoon the village on the Little Bighorn had perhaps half an hour's warning of the approach of soldiers. Had he known the truth, Custer might still have hidden the regiment, reconnoitered, and struck at dawn on June 26.

Custer drew reproach for dividing the regiment in the face of superior strength. That he faced superior strength, of course, he neither knew nor cared. He formed battalions because of the need to advance in a reconnaissance in force and doubtless also because of his intention, if possible, to attack from more than one direction.

The Failures of Reno and Benteen

The division of the regiment entailed unavoidable consequences for the impending battle. Because of their seniority

Custer had to give battalion commands to Reno and Benteen. Within limits of personal ability they could be expected to do their duty, but not with the enthusiastic, unquestioning loyalty of the favorites in the "royal family." Custer compounded the problem by keeping the most reliable officers with him. Of his inner circle only [Captain Thomas] Weir and [Captain Miles] Moylan rode with the other battalions.

Custer's decision to order Benteen to the left was sensible. He had to assure himself that the upper Little Bighorn contained no Indians who might fall on his rear in battle or escape southward, as Terry feared. Had the Indians continued up the valley as intended, Benteen would probably have spotted them. If not, the trail would have led to them, and another battle altogether would have resulted.

As it turned out, the scout to the left counted Benteen and three companies out of the critical stage of the battle. It need not have. Benteen counted himself out, as timing factors show. When he came back to the main trail, he was about half an hour behind Custer and Reno. When he neared the mouth of Reno Creek, he was one hour and twenty minutes behind. Had he moved at the same pace as Custer, and had he responded to the message brought by Martin [trumpeter John Martin, who brought a handwritten note from Custer's battalion just before the battle] with the swiftness that Custer expected, Benteen might well have fought with Custer. He and his battalion might have perished with Custer, too, but that does not excuse the laggard pace that kept one-fourth of the regiment out of the fight at a decisive moment.

Benteen's course is hard to understand. A possible explanation is distrust of Custer coupled with a rising suspicion that Custer, hoping to keep him out of the fight, had sent him on a useless errand. [Captain Miles] Keogh or [George] Yates would have signaled a gallop as soon as they received Seargent [Daniel] Kanipe's report.

Reno also failed Custer, as well as every test of leadership. His retreat freed large numbers of Indians to concentrate on Custer just as he reached the mouth of Medicine Tail Coulee. Had Reno continued to fight in the valley, the pressure on Custer would have been lessened, perhaps decisively. What cannot be known is whether such a course would have awarded Reno the same fate as Custer. Significantly, those who followed Reno into the valley did not condemn the decision to withdraw, only the execution. Some, however, did think that he could have stood firm in the timber, a belief shared by some of the Indian combatants.

Likewise vulnerable is Reno's management of the hilltop operation. He should have rushed to Custer's aid no matter what the odds and even at the risk of disaster to his own companies. The written orders to Benteen, now Reno's by virtue of superior rank, explicitly required such a move. In addition, some of his officers urged this course on him. In fact, Reno made no decision, and his indecision freed subordinates to go off on their own and in the end endangered the entire command. Thereafter, through a night and day of defensive action, he failed to exert effective command. Indeed, there is evidence that he proposed to pull out altogether, abandoning the wounded, a proposition that Benteen indignantly rejected. In fact, no one doubted that Benteen functioned as the true commander. His strong leadership and cool bravery contributed greatly to the successful defense.

On the Custer battlefield itself, nagging questions of leadership arise. Can Indian numbers alone account for Yates's quick repulse from the ford at the mouth of Medicine Tail Coulee? This movement shifted the initiative from the cavalry to the Indians and forced the battle into terrain inhospitable to mounted action. The retreat of both battalions to Battle Ridge also allowed warriors to thrust up Medicine Tail Coulee in strength and thus cut them off from the rest of the regiment.

On Battle Ridge, how to account for patterns of fallen bodies that suggest only one pocket of organized defense— L Company on Calhoun Hill? And how further to account for the concentration of company commanders on Custer Hill? George Yates, Tom Custer, and Algernon Smith fell here. Much of Yates's Company F appears to have died here, but most of C and E perished on other parts of the field.

Whatever Armstrong Custer's failings, combat leadership was not one. Did he take one or two mortal wounds at the Medicine Tail ford? Did that so demoralize Yates's men that they too readily allowed themselves to be driven back from the ford? This move, in turn, led Keogh to yield his position on the heights and fight his way northward to join them on Calhoun Hill. The dead Custer finally came to rest on Custer Hill. Either mortally wounded or dead, he could have been borne there from as far away as Medicine Tail Coulee. No one can ever know, but such a theory would account for much that is puzzling about the fighting on the Custer battlefield.

On the other hand, Adjutant [William W.] Cooke fell near at Custer rather than with Keogh, to the east. Had Custer ceased to function, command would have devolved on Keogh, and Cooke's place would have been with him. Also, there is some indication that expended shells from Custer's Remington sporting rifle were found near his body.

Even more compelling, this theory would force the American people to relinquish the glorious image of Custer's Last Stand that is indelibly burned into their collective memory. That renunciation is as unthinkable as it is impossible.

The Chances for a Victory

Could Custer have won? It is a question destined to be forever debated and never settled. Even against the Sioux and Cheyennes in all their numbers and power, however, good arguments support a conclusion that he could have won.

Crucial to this conclusion is the fact that Custer came close to surprising the Indians. The men had little time to prepare for battle. Most of the ponies grazed on the benchland. Several hundred warriors managed to mobilize to meet Reno, but most of the fighters in the village were not ready. Had there been warning, the men would surely have engaged Custer before he got close enough to endanger their families.

In such circumstances Indians usually panicked. Suddenly confronted with soldiers among their tipis, each man turned instinctively to the safety of his family. Thus distracted, the fighting strength could not offer organized resistance, and the village exploded in fleeing family groups. This could be expected to happen even when the Indians enjoyed superiority of numbers.

At the Little Bighorn several scenarios held the possibility of producing such a panic.

First, and most simply, a charge by the eight companies of Custer and Reno into the upper [southern] end of the village would almost certainly have stampeded the Indians. The force and momentum of a mounted charge by nearly 350 cavalrymen would have carried into the very heart of the village, striking consternation and chaos and preventing the formation of effective defenses. The attackers would have taken severe casualties, and most of the Indians would have escaped to the north, but Custer would have been left in possession of the village and possibly of much of the pony herd. Benteen and the packtrain would have come up in time to fortify the victors.

Even the two-pronged attack that Custer must have visualized might have worked had Reno not lost his nerve. To continue his charge into the village with 112 men required a fortitude and blind loyalty to Custer that Reno, unlike Keogh or Yates, did not possess. Such an assault, however, could have created enough momentary confusion to win success *if* Custer had driven into the village at the Medicine Tail ford before the Indians could recover and swallow Reno's small command. To achieve this feat, Custer would have had to cover more than three miles, from the bluffs where he overlooked the valley to the mouth of Medicine Tail Coulee, before the Indians crushed Reno. The possibilities of this formula seem slim.

More plausible is Reno holding the timber long enough for Custer to get into the village at the Medicine Tail ford. Although control was difficult in the timber, Reno had taken few casualties when he ordered the retreat. In forming the skirmish line, two horses had bolted and carried their riders into the Sioux. One man had died on the skirmish line and two in the timber. One of the latter was the Ree scout Bloody Knife, sitting on his horse beside Reno. A bullet struck his head and spattered blood and brains into Reno's face, an unnerving experience that contributed to the decision to get out of the timber. Had Reno's force remained in place, the warriors here could not have left for Medicine Tail without exposing their families. As it happened, Reno's withdrawal freed them to concentrate on Custer in a strength that forced him back from the river into unfriendly terrain.

Could Benteen have altered the outcome? A swift march on Custer's trail upon receiving Kanipe's report probably would have brought him to Medicine Tail while the action still centered there. His presence might at least have allowed Custer to extricate himself and consolidate the entire regiment on Reno Hill. Had Reno held in the valley, Benteen's timely appearance on Medicine Tail would have given Custer eight companies with which to storm into the village and perhaps carry the day.

The fourth scenario is less a prescription for victory than a remote possibility of staving off defeat. Had Reno and Benteen corralled the packtrain and the wounded on the bluff tops and boldly rushed six companies to the sound of the firing, could they have saved Custer? With a brand of leadership neither had yet displayed, they might have averted the total annihilation of Custer's command. But they would have been badly mauled themselves, perhaps even wiped out. This course should have been tested more promptly and vigorously than it was, but a favorable outcome seems improbable.

Besides the Seventh Cavalry's officers, other campaign leaders are open to criticism but have remained largely immune because of the storm swirling around Custer. Neither before nor after the Little Bighorn did Terry, Gibbon, or Crook gather and use intelligence in a thoughtful way. Gibbon let opportunity slip from his grasp and failed to keep Terry even minimally informed. Crook mismanaged both his March and June offensives, withdrawing on both occasions with dubious justification. The second withdrawal, after the Rosebud, stopped his movement into the very country that Custer entered less than a week later. Had Crook continued his advance, he could not have failed to alter the result of Custer's offensive. Privately, General [William T.] Sherman believed that Crook bore large responsibility for the failure of the campaign.

And yet, in dissecting strategy and tactics from the perspective of a century later, it is easy to do injustice to the responsible commanders. One cannot know all the circumstances of enemy, weather, terrain, troops, weapons, and a host of other factors great and trivial (Gibbon had a bad stomachache) that influenced judgment and sometimes decisively shaped the final outcome.

But one conclusion seems plain. George Armstrong Custer does not deserve the indictment that history has imposed on him for his actions at the Little Bighorn. Given what he knew at each decision point and what he had every reason to expect of his subordinates, one is hard pressed to say what he ought to have done differently. In truth, at the Little Bighorn "Custer's Luck" simply ran out. Although the failures of subordinates may have contributed and the strength and prowess of the foe certainly contributed, Custer died the victim less of bad judgment than of bad luck.

3

Envy and Pique Motivated Captain Benteen

Larry Sklenar

Many historians believe that Custer made his worst mistake by dividing his forces just before the Battle of the Little Bighorn. Although he knew that a vast Indian encampment lay just across the Little Bighorn River, Custer decided to split up the Seventh Cavalry, a force that was already well outnumbered. Custer sent three troops of cavalry with Major Marcus Reno to the south side of Reno Creek, and ordered Reno to attack the camp from its southern limit. He sent another three troops with Captain Frederick Benteen on a reconnaissance across the hills to the west. Benteen was ordered to seek out any warriors attempting to leave the camp and escape the two-pronged attack that was about to take place. Unlike Reno and Custer, however, Benteen saw no action at all that day. Instead, he cut his mission short and pulled his forces up on the promontory known as Reno Hill, where Reno's and Benteen's commands fended off Indian attacks for thirty-six hours after the main battle had concluded.

Since the last of Custer's Seventh Cavalry troopers were buried in the hills above the Little Bighorn valley, the actions of Captain Benteen have come under close scrutiny by historians of the battle. Some have placed a large share of blame for Custer's Last Stand on Benteen's delay in coming to Custer's aid once the shooting started. Why, after having received an urgent handwritten message from Custer to "Come quick!" did Benteen decide to dally along Reno Creek? This has been a crucial question of all Little Bighorn studies since the battle took place.

Historian Larry Sklenar provides one possible answer in the following extract from his book *To Hell with Honor*. Although he finds Benteen to be a competent officer, Sklenar faults the captain for his petty jealousy of Custer's renown, and sees Benteen acting out of pique at being left out of the fighting by Custer. To Benteen, the reconnaissance ordered by Custer seemed nothing more than a worthless diversion and an attempt by Custer to hog the spoils of war for himself. Sklenar concludes that the petulant actions of an otherwise professional soldier helped bring about the Seventh Cavalry's worst defeat.

Once again, in Captain Frederick Benteen's mind, Custer had given him the hard work to do—the unrewarding work—even the dirty work. Feeling that he was being denied the opportunity to share in Custer's push for glory, Benteen went off in a pout to perform the bare necessities of duty. His annoyance at being left out of the main line of attack doubtless increased as his column plodded through terrain unsuited for Indian encampments and as his growing frustration with Custer's seemingly useless orders fed an overactive imagination. In the end, visions of Custer and Major Marcus Reno dashing to victory made him deaf to clear entreaties and impaired the judgment of an otherwise capable officer.

At about a quarter past noon on 25 June, as the Seventh Cavalry halted on the western side of the Divide [the high ground lying between the Rosebud and Little Bighorn Rivers], Custer summoned Benteen to give him the following instructions, as described by Benteen himself: *"He told me, pointing to a line of bluffs* [emphasis added], to go to that line of bluffs, or at first to send an officer with five or six men to ride *rapidly* [emphasis added] to that line of bluffs . . . and if I came across anything before I got to that line of bluffs to pitch into them and send word back to him at once." If Benteen found nothing, he was to return to the main trail. Benteen claimed at the court of inquiry that these were "exact orders, requiring no interpretation."

However, in communications outside the court, Benteen changed the nature of his assignment from reconnoitering the hills for signs of Indians to endless valley hunting. Before Benteen had gone very far, Custer supposedly sent two follow-up messages by way of Chief Trumpeter Henry Voss and Sergeant Major William Sharrow to the effect that if Benteen discovered no Indians at the first line of bluffs, he was to continue on to a second group of hills, then to a third. Whether those messengers actually conveyed such instructions can never be known with certainty. It does seem strange that Voss and Sharrow would have carried identical directives when one message "to keep on going" would have done as well, but the historical record is stuck with Benteen's word, however tainted by his lack of candor on a host of other issues.

To some extent Benteen gave the game away in letters to his wife shortly after the battle. Without admitting directly the existence of a Custer plan, Benteen hinted at the truth, which he would subsequently stretch into a pointless excursion. "I was ordered with my battalion to go over the immense hills to the left, *in search of the valley* [the valley of the Little Bighorn], *which was supposed to be very nearby* [emphasis added]—and to pitch into anything I came across,—and to inform Custer at once if I found anything worthy of same." Obviously, if there were lines of bluffs to be investigated, there were valleys between them, and those valleys might conceal Indian encampments, but nowhere except in Benteen's subsequent rationalizations did Custer's orders entail a search for the valley of the Little Bighorn.

When Custer pointed to the hills several miles in the distance, he knew two things for certain: the main Indian village lay concealed in the Little Bighorn bottomland some twelve miles away; and there was a smaller encampment a bit more than half as far from the place where he stood on the downslope of the Divide—or, to use Benteen's language, "nearby." That smaller Sans Arc satellite village was the first military objective. Lieutenant Winfield Edgerly heard Custer tell Reno to advance toward that village. Since Edgerly was a subordinate in Benteen's battalion, and since he heard those orders to Reno, the likelihood is that Benteen heard them also. But more important, Edgerly understood that the mission of Benteen's unit was to engage those Sans Arcs if they attempted to escape to the left, or south. Although collateral in nature and undertaken without surgeons, Benteen's task formed an essential part of the overall plan to attack that Indian encampment and, if possible, to take some prisoners. It is inconceivable that Benteen was not privy to at least that much of Custer's thinking.

And Benteen did understand the potential value of acquiring some Indian captives, as he told his wife. He noted that if Custer had not disobeyed General Alfred Terry's orders, such an outcome might have been realized. "Had Custer carried out [the] order he got from Genl. Terry the command would have formed a junction exactly at the village—and have captured the whole outfit of tepees, etc, and probably any quantity of squaws, pappooses, etc. etc. but Custer disobeyed orders from the fact of not wanting any other command—or body to have a finger in the pie." Benteen used a similar expression to his wife several weeks later, when he criticized General George Crook for failing to join Terry after the Little Bighorn fight so that the combined columns could chase the Indian survivors. Benteen believed that Crook "had held aloof from it—he wanting all the pie for himself." Everyone, it seems, wanted to swipe Benteen's slice of dessert. . . .

Benteen Turns Back Toward Custer

The total distance covered in Benteen's trip from the Divide to the hills and back to the main trail was likely a bit more than seven miles, taking about two and a half hours. Rather than hustling the fast walking horses forward at four miles an hour, which was suggested by various officers and which would have been closer to Custer's order to move rapidly, Benteen's battalion traveled at under three miles an hour—a brooding pace even after allowance is made for the terrain and possible delays while [Lieutenant Francis] Gibson made several trips to the peaks of nearby hills. Benteen later declared under oath that the gait of his fast walking horse was five miles an hour. "That accounts for getting over so much ground in so short a time," he insisted. His command went in "hot haste" both ways, he contended. However, by way of comparison, the Custer and Reno columns had covered essentially the same distance in an hour less time. . . .

It was a little before three o'clock when Benteen's battalion emerged near the mouth of No Name Creek, at which point the column was about four miles behind the separated Custer and Reno components. A hard-riding courier could easily have overtaken Custer in less than an hour, but Benteen was in no mood to chase the man who had left him behind. Rather, after a short ride down Reno Creek, Benteen decided to water the horses.

In the mostly dry land, it was incumbent on Benteen to provide succor to thirsty animals fatigued by a dusty march of almost three hours through hilly country. Along the full length of Reno Creek, there were not many places where such relief could be found. The Morass (as it was afterward known) was one such place. Variously called a watering hole or a spring-fed hollow, the highly alkaline Morass must have been sufficiently large that it could accommodate a number of horses at one time, though the water level above mud could not have been great.

For perhaps as long as twenty minutes, Benteen allowed the horses to suck bad-tasting water out of that Morass. Benteen himself provided an almost playful description of his own mount's determined efforts to get at that borderline muck. While watering his horse, Benteen tied tricky old Dick to a stump to keep the fractious horse from getting away. It seems that this mount, like its master, had a mind of its own and, once loose, would rejoin the troop when it was good and ready.

Some of Benteen's subordinates were apparently less amused by the lengthy stay at the water hole. Amplifying on testimony given at the court of inquiry, [Lieutenant Edward] Godfrey told Walter Camp that Benteen remained at the Morass for so long that some of the officers began to grow uneasy. One unidentified subaltern wondered why the "Old Man" was keeping them for such a long time. Captain Thomas Weir especially became impatient with the delay and suggested to Benteen that the column "ought to be over there," indicating the direction from which firing could be heard. According to Godfrey, Weir started out with his company even though he was normally second in the line of march. Seeing Weir depart, Benteen ordered the rest of the column to advance.

If any of the men did actually hear shooting while at the Morass, its origin is unclear, but two enlisted men in H Troop confirmed that such firing could be heard. At this time, roughly 3:15–3:20, the only sources of gunfire were the opening shots of the Arikara scouts and their several Sioux opponents, about seven miles distant. Given Weir's penchant for following the military dictum "to go to the sound of the firing," perhaps a faint shot or two stimulated his independent movement. Or perhaps he was simply upset by the perceived waste of precious time while the bulk of the regiment was operating out of sight. But if gunfire was heard ahead of the battalion, then Benteen is even more guilty of dereliction of duty than is obvious from the record.

As Benteen and his column moved away from the Morass, the pack train occupied the vacated space, the mules driving headlong for the shallow pool of water. The frenzied animals lurched forward to satisfy their thirst, and at least one of them became completely mired in the mud while several others sank ankle-deep in the soft edges of the hole. Extracting the mules proved to be a nuisance for the civilian packers and the soldiers with the train; Lieutenant Edward Mathey stated that during this period, packs were once again "very much scattered from front to rear." Still, most witnesses agreed that the pack train was not at the Morass for more than twenty to thirty minutes.

Considering that the pack train had traveled only about a mile less than Benteen and had started from the Divide nearly half an hour later, its progress was satisfactory. By the clock, the whole train maintained a good pace of three miles an hour, even with some loads coming off and having to be repacked. The train remained at the Morass about as long as Benteen's battalion had, even though it was a larger component, had mules mired, and had to recover packs. . . .

Sergeant Kanipe Reaches Benteen's Command

With an unhappy Weir in the lead, Benteen's command probably made good time from the Morass to the Lone Tepee, a distance of about a mile. Benteen said the column moved at a "stiff walk." Reaching the burial lodge, Benteen dismounted to examine it. The structure had been set afire more than an hour earlier, and still Benteen could describe it as "a beautifully decorated tepee of buffalo hide," in which was housed a single Indian "on a scaffold or cot of rude poles," indicating that Custer's firing of the lodge had done little more than create a temporary smudge pot. After a brief visit, the column resumed its march toward the Little Bighorn, with Benteen back in the lead.

[Sergeant Daniel] Kanipe [Kanipe had been sent by Custer to relay instructions to Benteen] was consistent in stating that he actually met Benteen about a mile west of the

Lone Tepee. It was now 3:40–3:45, about the time Trumpeter John Martin was riding hard along Sharpshooter Ridge bearing Custer's second message to the rear components of the regiment. Galloping in the direction of the column that Kanipe may now have recognized as Benteen's, the sergeant removed his hat and waved it, in response to which the battalion turned to the right to meet him. Kanipe recalled that the command was marching in column of twos, without any separation.

The encounter between Kanipe and Benteen could not have taken more than a moment or two. As directed by Tom Custer, Kanipe informed Benteen that the train was to be hurried along straight across country, cutting off loose packs unless they contained ammunition. He added, "They want you up there as quick as you can get there—they have struck a big Indian camp."

That uncomplicated message by itself might have prompted Benteen to hurry his command with mules carrying ammunition in a direct line to Custer, but unfortunately for all, Kanipe conveyed another and inadvertent impression. Understandably excited, Kanipe was bringing word from the front to men at the back end of the enterprise, and he could not refrain from saying more than he knew for sure. All that he could have reported with certainty was that Reno's command was advancing toward the Indian village and that Custer's column was about to move out in a northern direction. He had seen no more than that. However, natural optimism had an inordinate influence over his tongue, and in the flush of completing one part of his assignment and wanting no doubt to encourage his comrades, he told them what they surely wanted to hear: "We've got 'em!"—echoing Custer's own disposition as he had ridden down from his first visit to Sharpshooter Ridge.

The primary source for Kanipe's extraneous comments is Lieutenant Godfrey's several descriptions of the event. Besides reporting the exclamation that the advance units had "got 'em," Godfrey quoted Kanipe as saying, "They are licking the stuffing out of them." From these kinds of comments, Godfrey concluded, those present inferred that Custer had captured the village. Such an interpretation of Kanipe's spoken words and animated body language was obviously wrong, but if Godfrey was really convinced of that point of view, then Benteen—the man who mattered most

Vast numbers of Sioux overwhelmed the 211 men of the Seventh Cavalry. Custer's strategy and the tactics of the Sioux continue to be debated.

and who was all too ready to think the worst of Custer—was a willing receptacle for the notion that his natural enemy had already won the day without him.

The depth of Benteen's petulant funk was demonstrated by his immediate dismissal of Kanipe without enough conversation to ascertain Custer's real situation and by his later unwillingness at times to even admit that Kanipe had brought him orders. The arrival of a buoyant Kanipe confirmed what Benteen had suspected since Custer had sent him on that pointless valley-hunting exercise: Custer wanted to keep him out of the fight. If Custer did not need him engaged in the main event, Benteen knew how to dawdle, fishing pole at the ready. For an officer as seasoned as Benteen to have refrained from interrogating Kanipe at length is proof enough of Benteen's mood. He could convince himself that the instructions were not intended for him, and besides, [Captain Thomas] McDougall's Company B—and by extension, the pack train with its ammunition—belonged to Custer's right wing.

The messenger's assertions aside (that he bore orders for Benteen to "come on quick"), Benteen stated to the court of inquiry that Kanipe carried only instructions to the commanding officer of the mule train to hurry up the packs. Benteen told the sergeant that he had nothing to do with that and that Kanipe could find Captain McDougall and the pack train some "seven miles" in the rear. "He simply had verbal instructions to the commanding officer of the pack train and I did not consider that an order to me," Benteen said again of Kanipe's brief visit. Benteen attested that the sole message meant for him was delivered later, by Trumpeter Martin.

The truth may be that except for Benteen's forced treatment of the subject at the court of inquiry, he was in denial regarding the seminal importance of Kanipe's visit. Kanipe was emphatic in his claim that he had carried a directive from Custer for Benteen to hurry and that he had delivered those instructions to Benteen in person. Benteen's contention that he received no such order might carry equal weight were it not for the fact that Kanipe diverted from his path with the obvious purpose of seeking out the captain to convey the instructions as Tom Custer had spoken them. Kanipe was guilty of saying too much to a prideful officer in a snit, but in sending the noncommissioned officer packing in search of the train, Benteen was forecasting his attitude toward a similarly effusive Trumpeter Martin.

Kanipe did not need Benteen's help in finding the pack train. He had had it under observation since he had started downhill from the position just short of Sharpshooter Ridge. The packs were not seven miles in the rear, as suggested by Benteen, but were only a mile or so back and were closing on the Lone Tepee. Assuming that Kanipe continued to ride at a courier's pace, it probably did not take him more than ten minutes to reach his destination, although he later indicated that the time seemed closer to twenty minutes. Kanipe claimed that after delivering the orders to Captain McDougall, he "rode at the head of the pack train and brought them back as near as" he could to the route he had followed in coming from Custer—that is, across country, as instructed. . . .

Trumpeter Martin's Message from Custer

While Kanipe was guiding the pack train over precisely the ground he had covered on his way from Sharpshooter Ridge, not directly across country as he later recollected, Trumpeter Martin arrived to deliver Custer's final message to Benteen. It was almost four o'clock. Reno had begun his retreat from the valley, and Custer was lingering in Medicine Tail Coulee, waiting for word from [scout] Mitch Boyer before dispatching the ghostly, larger-than-life gray horses down the gully to sow indecision in the minds of his adversaries.

After Godfrey's report of hearing gunfire while at the Morass, there was apparently no further evidence of a fight in progress, even though the Benteen column had moved at a steady pace of five miles an hour toward Reno's noisy withdrawal from the field. At about this time Trumpeter Martin arrived with Custer's last call for help. The mystery is that based on the trumpeter's report, no senior officer among Custer's reserves had the curiosity to investigate the true state of affairs or the gumption to take unsure steps in the direction of the action.

In one of his accounts, Martin said that he—like Kanipe—waved his hat as he raced downhill to intercept Benteen's column, with the commander himself riding at a fast trot in the lead. Weir and the rest of the battalion were several hundred yards to the rear. Responding to Benteen's request for Custer's location, Martin said that the Indians were running and he supposed that by then Custer had charged through the village. Martin meant to tell Benteen about Reno being in action as well, but before he could continue his story, Benteen changed the subject by noting that Martin's horse had been wounded.

In none of his renderings did Martin ever indicate that he pointed in the direction Custer had gone. Neither did he answer in words Benteen's understandable question about the regimental commander's location. In short, Benteen asked *where*, and Martin answered *what*, and that *what* was more than the orderly could have known positively. In everything that he said or did, Martin unintentionally created a false impression, but in truth, it would have been improper for any enlisted man to volunteer information to an officer. It was Benteen's responsibility to inquire into the matter until he was satisfied, but apparently he did not. Rather, with Custer's message in hand and with the Kanipe and Martin unintentional impressions in mind, Benteen was content to let his athletic imagination leap to the only possible conclusion: his "pre's" had been right again, and Custer had deliberately gone off in search of glory alone.

Benteen agreed that he met Martin about two miles from the river and some two and a half miles beyond the Lone Tepee, in the vicinity of the Flat. For a full mile (the distance from the Flat to Reno Hill), Benteen had seen the lone rider that was Martin approaching, appearing and disappearing down the rolling slope. That is, within about fifteen minutes of Kanipe's departure for the pack train, Benteen observed another courier hurrying down from the bluffs on the east side of the river valley.

Captain Benteen always contended that the orderly had used the word "skedaddling" to describe what the Indians in the village were doing, but Martin denied ever having employed such a term. Whether Martin used that expression or not, by his own admission he had suggested to Benteen that the Indians were running. The truth was probably encapsulated in a Benteen remark at the court of inquiry: "My impression from Trumpeter Martin was that the Indians were skedaddling." This may have been Benteen's word for what Martin had told him.

In one of his narratives, Benteen described Martin as "a thick headed, dull witted Italian, just about as much cut out for a cavalryman as he was for a King." Benteen's low opinion of the trumpeter-orderly may have been the consequence of daily dealings, but Benteen may also have held him responsible for a distorted report at a critical moment, just as Benteen probably faulted Lieutenant Gibson for an incomplete intelligence report during Custer's assault at the Lone Tepee site. Additionally, Martin's badly garbled testimony at the court of inquiry, especially if the trumpeter had been coached, probably did not endear him to Benteen.

Big village. Come quick. Bring packs. That was the essence of the message written out by Adjutant William Cooke and delivered by Martin. Nothing in the text or the postscript specified hurrying the ammunition packs forward, even though, as indicated, enlisted men and civilian packers knew that this cargo was so special that it needed to be kept out in front. Following the abbreviated conversation with Martin, Benteen read the message and handed it to Captain Weir, who had by this time ridden up to the head of the column. Weir also read the note and supposedly offered no comment, nor did Benteen ask any questions of his subordinate. The message was unambiguous in stating that Benteen was to "come quick" with the packs, but the quandary for the bewildered Benteen was how to do both things at once.

The slow-moving mule train was still more than a mile behind, and if Benteen waited, he could not "come quick"; if he went back to get it, precious time would be lost; if he continued forward at a rapid pace, the distance between the two components would increase. At the court of inquiry, Benteen argued his case on just such grounds, and it is hard to fault his logic, even though his argument was laced with a fair amount of rationalization and ended up sounding more like an excuse than a reason. He went on to explain that another courier (Kanipe) had already passed by with instructions for McDougall and the train to come straight across country. Although he recognized that it was his duty to bring up the packs after receiving the order by way of Martin, Benteen said that after the orderly had conveyed his "skedaddling" comment, "there was less necessity for . . . going back for the packs." In fact, Benteen added, Martin gave the impression that Custer had not only attacked and scattered the Indians but was "in possession of the village."

Like Custer before him, Benteen felt that he could advance without waiting for the packs because any enemy force would have to get through his battalion in order to reach the train. "Well!" Edgerly quoted him as saying, "If he [Custer] wants me in a hurry, how does he expect that I can bring the packs? If I am going to be of service to him, I think I had better not wait for the packs." In his official report Benteen said, "It savored too much of 'coffee-cooling' [i.e., playing it safe] to return when I was sure a fight was progressing in the front." Or as he told the court of inquiry, "I couldn't waste time in going back, nor in halting where I was for them." Finally, Benteen insisted that he had not sent Martin with any message to McDougall.

Late in his life, Martin stated flatly that he did not carry any instructions to the pack train. When he reached Benteen's position, the packs were in sight, but as the battalion sped up, McDougall's command and the packs faded to just another dust cloud. The problem with this version of Martin's recollection is that it totally contradicts the very detailed testimony he gave at the court of inquiry.

He told the court that as he approached the train, the packs were pretty well closed up and McDougall was riding 150 yards to the rear of the column. Martin informed McDougall that Benteen "sent his compliments and wanted him to hurry up the packs." Martin then rode back and took his place on the left of his assigned company (H) in Benteen's battalion. This testimony is compelling because it was given under oath and included particulars such as McDougall's position in the column and the language of a courier delivering instructions. Additionally, this was what Benteen ought to have done in order to be in compliance with Custer's orders.

On the other hand, Edgerly claimed that he heard Martin speak to another cavalryman behind Benteen. Martin was laughing and seemed very much elated, saying that it was the biggest village he had ever seen and that Reno had charged and was killing all of the inhabitants. Edgerly supposed that Benteen heard Martin's overzealous and wrongheaded excesses. At a minimum, Martin did not leave immediately with a message for the pack train.

The evidence is skimpy and conflicting, but the probability is that Martin did not carry a message to McDougall and the pack train. Instead, he was given another horse and joined his company and rode on, no doubt continuing to babble excitedly to his comrades about his singular experience. If we therefore accept Martin's disavowal of his court of inquiry testimony, one is left to wonder what might have prompted the young enlisted man to deliberately lie under oath. Martin claimed that the court record was a mistake, but on this issue the questions were too precise and Martin's replies too fulsome to reflect mere errors in transcription.

And so Benteen apparently started forward without sending any additional notification to the pack train. His subordinates agreed with him. As Edgerly said, "The remark was made by someone, either by Captain Weir or myself, that he [Custer] could not possibly want us to go for the packs as Captain McDougall was there and would bring them up." Although Edgerly wanted to go faster, he concurred in the deliberate gait in order to keep the horses in good condition. Godfrey thought that the command marched at a walk or a trot, depending on the terrain—the same ground over which Custer's column had advanced without apparent difficulty and, more important, over which Reno's battalion had moved toward the river at an overall speed of a fast trot. . . .

It is hard to imagine that Benteen did not get Martin to tell him on which side of the river he might find Custer's command. Such a lame excuse for not going directly toward Custer ought to have gotten Benteen laughed out of the court of inquiry, but it did not. An ordinarily inquisitive person would have extracted more information out of Kanipe and Martin than did this supposedly experienced officer, for whom current and reliable intelligence ought to have been a fundamental concern. Beyond that, both of these enlisted men were within easy recall for use as guides had not Benteen's wounded pride blinded him to their potential value. Instead, he merely marched forward until faced with a dilemma, in a situation almost as comical—if it were not so tragic—as his patently ridiculous assertion that he was confused because Martin had failed to point him in the right direction. Custer sallied forth on an unknown trail, said Benteen, "and in a direction that we never guessed that he had gone until so informed by Chief Gall ten years after the occurrence of the battle."

The only valid presentiment probably experienced by Benteen was his decision to retain the original copy of Custer's orders, as written out by Adjutant Cooke. In a letter sent to his wife two weeks after the battle, Benteen suggested that she preserve the note—as well as the letter itself—"as the matter may be of interest hereafter, likewise for use." He knew then that someone would have to answer for the debacle at the Little Bighorn, and he was already beginning to prepare his case. Those letters to his wife constituted the framework on which he would later construct his defense, and the hastily written and poorly worded note was the exclamation point for his persistent denial of all responsibility.

By making himself tiny in the total scheme of things, Benteen was in fact able to avoid any official culpability for what happened to Custer and his command. Strictly speaking, he was *not* responsible for the pack train, even though it must have been widely understood that on the verge of battle, additional ammunition was the only cargo of any possible use to forces about to be or already engaged. The men with the packs knew that, Kanipe confirmed it, and the subject was implicit in Cooke's note—a realization that must have come to Benteen soon after the fact, for which reason he retained the note.

As adept as Benteen may have been in anticipating future difficulties, he was equally expert in analyzing contingencies after the fact. According to one of his correspondents, the illustrious captain later said that after the regiment reached the Little Bighorn, all packs except those carrying ammunition were of no further use. At that point, said Benteen, it would have made sense to abandon the mule train. This would have released 170 men for combat and, combined with Benteen's battalion, would have constituted a force of 290 soldiers. Benteen's numbers were wrong, but as he believed, such an assembly of forces could have cleared the valley had Reno held out in the timber.

Unfortunately, such a plan did not occur to Benteen when the occasion called for action, when everyone in the body of the regiment understood that projecting the ammunition packs to the forefront at critical junctures was an operational imperative, and when repeated messages from Custer expressed just that need. Of course, Benteen's purpose in proposing such a commonsense plan after the fact was to blame Custer for not thinking of it and to highlight Reno's cowardice. But the messages delivered by Sergeant Kanipe and Trumpeter Martin offered the perfect opportunities for Benteen not only to implement his ingenious afterthought but also to obey orders received from his commander.

Like Lieutenant Edgerly, Benteen understood his role in at least the first phase of Custer's battle plan, and Benteen probably knew that his battalion fell under Reno's left wing in any subsequent action. In all respects, Benteen possessed sufficient knowledge to have done the right thing, to have at least made some effort to provide assistance—with the ammunition—in a timely fashion to units already committed to battle. But for all the men who failed in ways that Benteen could fathom clearly in hindsight, he had only clenched teeth, a slightly curled lip, and scurrilous sniping in postbattle correspondence. One suspects that Benteen did sneer a little when he saw Boston Custer racing across the landscape to catch up with his older brothers before the fight began. The unbridled exuberance of the younger Custer, a receding figure swallowed by the tortured landscape, was the innocence lost on Benteen's march to the left.

For Further Research

Louise Barnett, *Touched by Fire: The Life, Death, and Mythic Afterlife of George Armstrong Custer.* New York: Henry Holt, 1996.

E.A. Brininstool and J.W. Vaughn, *Troopers with Custer: Historic Incidents of the Battle of the Little Big Horn.* Mechanicsburg, PA: Stackpole Books, 1994.

Roger Darling, *General Custer's Final Hours: Correcting a Century of Misconceived History.* Vienna, VA: Potomac-Western Press, 1992.

Brian W. Dippie, *Custer's Last Stand: The Anatomy of an American Myth.* Lincoln: University of Nebraska Press, 2002.

Richard A. Fox, *Archaeology, History, and Custer's Last Battle: The Little Big Horn Reexamined.* Norman: University of Oklahoma Press, 1993.

John S. Gray, *Custer's Last Campaign: Mitch Boyer and the Little Bighorn Reconstructed.* Lincoln: University of Nebraska Press, 1993.

Jay Monaghan, *Custer: The Life of General George Armstrong Custer.* Lincoln: University of Nebraska Press, 1959.

Peter F. Panzeri, *Little Big Horn 1876: Custer's Last Stand.* Oxford: Osprey, 1999.

Jerry L. Russell, *1876 Facts About Custer and the Battle of the Little Big Horn.* Mason, IA: Savas, 1999.

Edgar I. Stewart, *Custer's Luck.* Norman: University of Oklahoma Press, 1955.

Robert M. Utley and Brian W. Dippie, *Custer and the Great Controversy: The Origin and Development of a Legend.* Lincoln: University of Nebraska Press, 1998.

Herman J. Viola, *Little Bighorn Remembered: The Untold Indian Story of Custer's Last Stand.* New York: Times Books, 1999.

Jeffrey D. Wert, *Custer: The Controversial Life of George Armstrong Custer.* New York: Simon and Schuster, 1996.

Charles Windolph and Robert Hunt, *I Fought with Custer: The Story of Sergeant Windolph, Last Survivor of the Battle of the Little Big Horn.* Lincoln: University of Nebraska Press, 1987.

Index

Adams, Mary, 113
agencies, 14
    corruption in, 29
    "hostiles" vs., 98, 99
    Sitting Bull requested help from, 100
    see also Sioux
alcohol, 33, 39–40, 58, 65–66, 80
Ambrose, Stephen E., 77
    on *Far West* council of war, 104–106
    on march to Little Bighorn, 108–10
    on prophecy of Sitting Bull, 101–104
    on the Sioux, 98
    on Terry's orders to Custer, 106–108
American Horse, 62–64
Arikaras, 86–87

battalions, division of, 17
    Ambrose on, 110
    Cheyenne account of, 72
    Reno on, 52
    Sklenar on, 121
    Utley on, 115
Battle of Rosebud Creek, 15, 32, 74, 76, 101–104
    Cheyenne account of, 62
    Custer humiliated by, 112
    Lone Tepee and, 32, 52, 126, 129, 131
    Sioux/Cheyenne reaction at, 89–90
Battle of the Little Bighorn
    aftermath of, 84–87
    archaeological evidence from, 80–82
    Benteen's position during, 124–29
    Cheyenne warning of, 62–64
    conflict between Benteen and Custer, 122–24
    historical importance of, 18, 31–32
    Indians' preparation for, 73–75
    maps of, 16, 54
    military strategy, 55, 77, 90–91, 115, 118
    New York Times accounts of, 20–27
    orders from Custer to Benteen during, 129–35
    preparation for, 108–10
    timing of, 77, 90–91, 115, 118
    victory theory about, 118–20
    see also Indians; treaties; weapons;
        *individual names of Indians and U.S.
        Army officers*

Battle of the Washita, 10–11
Battle Where the Girl Saved Her
    Brother, 90
    see also Battle of Rosebud Creek
Belknap, William, 26
Benteen, Frederick, 15
    battle could have been altered by, 119
    conflict with Custer, 122–24
    Custer's orders to, 129–35
    position during battle, 17, 40, 124–29
    Reno on position of, 52, 58
    Utley's views on, 115–18
    Whittaker on, 49–50
Big Beaver, 83
Bighead, Kate, 80, 83–84
Bismarck Tribune (newspaper), 25
    see also Kellogg, Mark
Black Elk, 85–87, 90, 92, 95
Black Hills expedition, 25–27, 61, 88
Black Kettle, 11
Black Moon, 102
Bloody Knife, 55–56, 86–87, 105, 110, 119
Box Elder, 76
Boyer, Mitch, 74, 83, 109, 130
Bozeman Trail, 13
Brave Bear, 84, 95
Brave Wolf, 64
Brown, Dee, 88
    on death of Custer, 94–96
    on Reno's attack, 91–94
    views on Crazy Horse, 89–90
    on village of Little Bighorn, 90–91
Buffalo-Calf-Road-Woman, 90
Bullock, Alexander H., 29
Bury My Heart at Wounded Knee
    (Brown), 88

Calhoun, James, 24–25, 44, 69
Calhoun Hill, 82, 117
Canada, 29, 44
cannibalism, 85
Cavalier in Buckskin (Utley), 111
Cheyenne, 61–62
    Battle of the Washita, 10–11
    pursued Custer's troops, 79
    on surprise attack, 62–64
    views of Battle of the Little Bighorn, 65–72, 89–90, 93–96

see also individual Indian names
Cheyenne Memories of the Custer Fight (Grinnell), 61
Chief-Comes-in-Sight, 89–90
Coleman, James, 39
Contrary Belly, 68, 70–71
Cook, William W., 44, 56–57, 78, 118
    death of, 47
    message to Benteen, 131–34
    Reno on orders from, 52–53
Court of Inquiry, 39–40, 50, 131
Crazy Horse, 13–15, 75, 80, 89–90
Crazy Horse and Custer (Ambrose), 98
Crittendon, John J., 69
Crook, George, 14–18, 74, 90, 120
    Benteen's criticism of, 124
    retreat by, 76
    Sitting Bull's prophecy and, 102
    see also Battle of Rosebud Creek
Crow King, 93–95
Crowley, Cornelius, 33, 35
Crow scouts. *See* Indian scouts
Crow's Nest, 74
Curly, 42–45
Custer, Boston, 24–25, 46, 82, 135
Custer, Elizabeth Bacon. *See* Custer, Libbie
Custer, George Armstrong, 11–12, 81, 84, 104–105
    approach to Little Bighorn by, 113–15
    Battle of the Washita, 10–11
    Benteen and, 116, 122–24, 129–35
    Black Hills expedition of, 26
    Bloody Knife and, 87
    cavalry divided by, 17, 52, 72, 110, 115, 121
    characterized by *Harper's Weekly*, 28–30
    Cheyenne account of battle with, 63–64
    command discovered by Indians, 74–75, 110
    death of, 42–43, 45–46, 69–70, 94–95, 117–18
    Indians took weapons from, 65
    orders from Terry, 106–108, 111–13
    refused escape plan, 43
    refused extra troops, 15–16, 40
    Reno and, 103–104
    Reno on defeat of, 57–59
    see also Battle of the Little Bighorn
Custer, Libbie, 107
Custer, Thomas W., 82
    death of, 24–25, 45–46, 70
    instructions to Kanipe, 127, 129
Custer Hill, 82–83
Custer's Last Stand. *See* Battle of the Little Bighorn; Custer, George

Armstrong
"Custer's Luck," 75, 78, 111, 120

Dade, Frances, 26–27
Dakota column, 50, 75
    see also Terry, Alfred
democrats
    Custer family as, 11
    Democratic Convention, 109
Dorman, Isaiah, 87
Drum, R.C., 22

Edgerly, Winfield, 123–24, 133
Edwards, Arthur, 39

farming, 93
Far West (steamboat), 113
    Curly on, 42
    Terry's headquarters on, 15, 104–106
Flat Hip, 95
Foolish Elk, 83–84
Fort Laramie agreement, 13
Fox, Richard, 80–82

Gall, 79–80, 86–87, 93–94, 134
Gibbon, John, 14, 120
    Custer and, 50
    motivation of, 104–105
    planned reinforcement to Custer from, 75
    position at Rosebud, 102–103
    reinforcement by, 23
Gibson, Francis, 124, 131
Girard, Fred, 59, 77
Godfrey, Edward S., 108, 125, 127, 133
Graham, W.A., 51
Grant, Ulysses S., 28, 50, 112
graves, 82
Gray Horse Company, 68–72, 83
Grinnell, George Bird, 61
    interviews of
        American Horse, 62–64
        Brave Wolf, 64
        Soldier Wolf, 65–66
        Tall Bull, 66–67
        Two Moons, 71–72
        White Bull, 65
        White Shield, 67–70

Half Yellow Face, 59
hardtack incident, 74–76
Hare, Luther, 34, 57
Harper's Weekly (magazine), 28–30
Harshay Wolf, 85
Hawk, 84
Hayes, Rutherford B., 51
Hodgson, Benjamin, 33, 37, 53–56
horses

during battle, 33
at Battle of the Washita, 11
Gray Horse Company, 68–72, 83
used by Indians, 79–80
Hump, 94
Hunkpapas, 75–76, 90

Indians, 26–27, 35
Battle of the Washita, 10–11
death toll at Little Bighorn, 43, 66
number of, at Little Bighorn, 49–50,
78–79, 90–91
Reno on battle strategy of, 55
rituals of, 101–104
scouts warned Custer about number
of, 105, 110, 114
strength of, 112
surprised by attack, 17, 62–64,
75–78, 118
used horses in battle, 79–80
U.S. government policy on, 28–30
see also treaties
see also Cheyenne; Indian scouts;
Sioux; *individual Indian names*
Indian scouts, 105
angry about use of fire, 109
Curly, 42–45
Herndon, 49
Reno's account of, 53, 59
saw smoke on June 25, 74
warned Custer about number of
Indians, 105, 110, 114
see also Bloody Knife
Iron Hawk, 85
Iron Thunder, 92

Kanipe, Daniel, 116, 126–29, 132
Kellogg, Mark, 25, 104, 106, 109
Keogh, Miles, 87, 116, 118
Kill Eagle, 44, 94
Killing Custer (Welch), 73
Kinzie, John, 22

Last Stand. *See* Battle of the Little
Bighorn; Custer, George Armstrong
L Company, 117
Lincoln, Abraham, 12
Little Bighorn (valley), map of, 16, 54
Little Bighorn (village), 90–91
see also Battle of the Little Bighorn
Little Hawk, 70–71
Lone Tepee, 32, 52, 126, 129, 131
Long Hair Custer, 91
see also Custer, George Armstrong
Low Dog, 92, 95

maps
of Battle of the Little Bighorn, 54
of Little Bighorn and vicinity, 16

Marquis, Thomas B., 84
Martin, John. *See* Martini, Giovanni
Martini, Giovanni, 78, 116, 127,
129–35
Mathey, Edward, 126
McClellan, George, 12
McDougall, Thomas, 128, 129, 132–33
M Company, 52
Medicine Bear, 85
Medicine Tail Coulee, 117, 119, 130
military strategy
Reno on strategy of Indians, 55
for timing attacks, 77, 90–91, 115,
118
see also weapons; *individual names of
battles*
Minneconjous, 94, 95
Montana column, 75
see also Gibbon, John
Morass, 125
Moylan, Miles, 54, 55, 116
M Troop, 38
mutilation, 45, 85–86
Myers, "Tinker Bell," 38

Nebraska, 29, 98, 99
Neeley, Frank, 38
New York Herald (newspaper), 104
New York Times (newspaper), 20
on causes/consequences of battle,
25–27
confirmation of battle, 21–23
details of battle, 23–25
early reports of battle, 20–21
No Name Creek, 124
Northwestern Christian Advocate
(newspaper), 39

Oglalas, 90

Pizi. *See* Gall
Plains Indians, 12
see also Cheyenne; Indians; Sioux
Pleasanton, Alfred, 12
Powder River, 75, 98, 99
prophecies, 76, 101–104
Pte-San-Waste-Win, 91, 94

Rain-in-the-Face, 45, 95
Red Cloud, Jack, 99, 100
Red Cloud (chief), 27, 29, 99, 100
Red Horse, 91, 95
Reed, Autie, 46, 82
Reily, William Van W., 48–49
Reno, Marcus, 32, 34–37, 81, 91–94
alcoholic drinking by, 33, 39–40, 58
Cheyenne accounts of, 64–67
Curly's account of retreat by, 42–45
Custer and, 103–104

on defeat of Custer, 57–59
defied Terry's orders, 104
on his march to Little Bighorn,
  52–55
on his orders, 58–59
on his retreat to Reno Hill, 55–59
Indian attack on, 23–25, 63–64
at Rosebud Creek, 15
surprise attack by, 17, 75–78
Taylor's views on, 38–40
Utley's views on, 115–19
Whittaker's views on, 49–50
witnessed death of Bloody Knife,
  55–56, 86, 119
Reno Court of Inquiry, The (Graham),
  51
reservations. *See* agencies
Rising Sun, 87

sabres, 45
Sans Arcs, 90, 100–101, 123–24
Seventh Cavalry
  competition among officers of, 15
  Fox on, 80–82
  items belonging to, 87
  see also Battle of the Little Bighorn;
    Benteen, Frederick; Custer, George
    Armstrong; Reno, Marcus; Terry,
    Alfred
Sharrow, William, 123
Sheridan, Philip, 10, 12, 21–23, 26,
  114
Sheridan, William T., 21–23
Sherman, William T., 25–26, 120
Sioux
  Battle of the Washita, 10–11
  characterized by *New York Times*,
    26–27
  encampment by, 14
  Fort Laramie agreement with, 13
  "hostile," 98
  migration before battle, 98–101
  presence at Crow's Nest, 74
  U.S. Army expedition and, 14–18
  views of Battle of the Little Bighorn,
    88–93
  see also Indians; *individual Indian
    names*
Sitting Bull, 13–14, 75
  New York Times articles about, 21–23
  position of, 91
  prophecy of, 101–104
  requested help from agencies, 100
  role in battle, 95–96
Sitting Bull: Champion of the Sioux
  (Vestal), 85
Sklenar, Larry, 121–22
  on Benteen's orders from Custer,
    129–35

on Benteen's position during battle,
  124–29
on conflict between Benteen and
  Custer, 122–24
Smith, Algernon E., 44, 48, 69
Smith, John, 39
Soldier Wolf, 65–66
South Skirmish Line, 83
Spotted Tail, 99, 100
Stands in Timber, John, 86
suicide, 83–84

Tall Bull, 66–67
Taylor, William O., 31–32, 38–40
  on march to Little Bighorn, 33–34
  on Reno's battalion, 32–33
  on retreat by Reno, 34–38
Terry, Alfred, 120
  council on *Far West*, 104–106
  missing men reported to, 44
  orders from Grant, 50
  orders to Custer, 106–108, 111–13
  orders to Reno, 59
  planned reinforcement to Custer, 75
  Sioux expedition and, 14–18
Three Stars, 90
  see also Crook, George
To Hell with Honor (Sklenar), 122
treaties, 12–13
  of 1868, 93, 99
  Fort Laramie agreement, 13
  Harper's Weekly on violations of,
    29–30
  violated by Black Hills expedition,
    26–27
Turtle Rib, 83
Two Moons, John, 71–72, 85, 93–94

U.S. government
  army, 14–18
    see also Battle of the Little Bighorn
  policy toward Indians, 28–30, 88, 99
  see also treaties; *individual names of
    presidents*
Utley, Robert M., 111
  on Custer's actions, 113–15, 118–20
  on Reno and Benteen, 115–18
  on Terry's orders to Custer, 111–13

Varnum, Charles A., 17, 109, 110
Vestal, Stanley, 85
Voss, Henry, 123

Wallace, George D., 53
weapons
  archaeological evidence of, 81–82
  Custer's orders about, 110
  obtained by Indians from Custer's
    troops, 65

pack train with ammunition, 128,
    132–35
shooting and Benteen's troops,
    125–26
used by Custer, 45, 70, 118
used by Indians, 96
Weir, Thomas, 116, 125, 126, 130–31
Welch, James, 73
    on archaeological evidence of battle,
        80–82
    on battle aftermath, 84–87
    on Custer's order to Benteen for
        reinforcement, 78–80
    on final minutes of battle, 82–84
    on preparation by Indians, 73–75
    on Reno's attack, 75–78
White Bull, 65, 80, 83, 84–85, 95

White Shield, 67–70
Whittaker, Frederick, 41, 50–51
    on Custer's troops, 46–49
    on death of Custer, 45–46
    interview of Curly the Upsaroka
        scout, 42–45
With Custer on the Little Bighorn
    (Taylor), 31–32
Wooden Leg, 83, 85, 91

Yates, George, 44, 116
    on Calhoun Hill, 79
    death of, 24–25, 47–48
    movement at Medicine Tail Coulee,
        117
Yellow Nose, 68–71